Book Yourself Solid: 34 Secrets Every Orthodontist Must Know

Jimmy Nicholas
GKIC Marketer of the Year

Foreword by Dustin S. Burleson, D.D.S.

ISBN-13: 978-1978288263
ISBN-10: 1978288263

Book Yourself Solid: 34 Secrets Every Orthodontist Must Know /
Jimmy Nicholas. -- 1st ed.

DEDICATION

To my clients, who have trusted me to help them design a website that turns them into the go-to practice in their area. I never take that for granted. I jump out of bed every day excited about the opportunity to serve you.

I am RELENTLESS about YOUR success!

Businesses get in trouble when they neglect small problems. If a window in a building is broken and left unrepaired, soon all the windows will be shattered, creating a perception of chaos. The same principle applies to business. Attention to detail demonstrates corporate competence — and that the company cares about the consumer.

Michael Levine
Broken Windows, Broken Business

CONTENTS

FOREWORD

Some people want to write a book. Jimmy Nicholas had to write this book. It would be almost criminal to have his depth of knowledge about how an orthodontist can drastically boost his or her practice's bottom line — while enjoying more freedom — and not share it. He really is that good.

How do I know? Because I'm an orthodontist who hired Jimmy Nicholas. My name is Dr. Dustin Burleson, and I'm a speaker, teacher, author and founder of Burleson Orthodontics. In the first month after Jimmy revamped my website, I earned more than $103,000 in patient production from Google. Even if that's all he had accomplished for me, it would have been enough. But he helped me overhaul my entire marketing approach, and my orthodontics practice is more successful than I ever dreamed possible. In fact, as of the publishing of this book, last month alone, Jimmy's on-line marketing generated over $282,000 in patient production for my practices.

I met Jimmy through GKIC, the largest direct-response organization in the world and the brainchild of industry legend Dan Kennedy. In 2013, we were competing for GKIC Marketer of the Year Award and Jimmy kicked my butt. After he deservedly won, we became great friends and frequent Mastermind collaborators.

Jimmy pictured to the left and me to the right after Jimmy was announced the winner of the Marketer of the Year.

At the time, he was working wonders within the podiatry niche by tripling his clients' leads on the web. When I asked him whether his system might work for orthodontists, he said, "I don't know, but we can try." Immediately, I thought that was very different for a marketing person to be so honest. I knew Jimmy understood that marketing is all about testing. Every other so-called marketing expert I have ever had talked up the fact that their system would definitely work. Jimmy's honest approach was so refreshing to hear.

Jimmy knows that testing is essential when it comes to marketing, and he wasn't about to offer his expertise to a new group of clients without knowing for sure that he could deliver the same astonishing results. I coach and consult over 1,900 orthodontists in more than 23 countries. So I referred Jimmy to one of my coaching clients. After Jimmy completely reworked the practice's messaging, website and online marketing, the orthodontist went from virtually no web leads to 19, which turned into 14 appointments, within the first 45 days of launching his site. To this day, the web is one of the top new patient referral sources for this orthodontist.

Then, Jimmy did the same thing for me.

He doesn't get results by tiptoeing around clients or making half-hearted suggestions. Jimmy gives it to you straight, which is the only way to get the kind of outcomes he's known for. He has figured out not only what works for helping orthodontists predictably attract more new patients from the web, but he has also pioneered a system to help clients uncover their unique selling points. When you put those two things together, the results are mind-blowing.

I'm not going to tell you how much I paid for Jimmy's help. But it was a lot, and that was the "good friend" rate! Suffice it to say, you're getting the deal of a lifetime with this book. Use it to the fullest. Devour what's inside, apply everything, and watch what happens. One of the best things you can do for your business and your own peace of mind is to invest in a proven marketing system which automatically attracts more new patients into your practice. Personally, I think every orthodontist should hire Jimmy. But since he's only got so many hours in the day, this book is the next best option to having direct access to him.

Could your practice use the same $100,000 extra per month, or $200,000 extra per month, or even more like his system got for my practices? That's more than $1.2 million a year to $2.4 million a year, or even more that you aren't pulling in currently. Now, do I know with a 100% certainty that you will experience the same results from Jimmy's 3-step system that I did? Of course not… I would give the same answer Jimmy gave me when I asked him a similar question, "I don't know." We both know marketing is all about testing. I also know Jimmy's system has helped our practices tremendously. His system has also profitably helped many of my orthodontic private coaching clients who I have referred to his team.

From what I know today, there is very little risk in testing his proven 3-step system in your practice. Additionally, your potential reward is so high. I would not recommend implementing the 3-step on your own or with any other marketing company other than Jimmy Marketing. Jimmy has formed and leads a highly-skilled and professional team of marketing specialists. As I have seen Jimmy Marketing grow and help more clients, Jimmy is constantly bringing in more and more specialists which makes their service and results even better as they grow.

I highly recommend you read every page of this book and then quickly reach out to Jimmy Marketing to learn more about their process and see if you think their 3-step system would work for you. Do not miss out like some of my clients have because Jimmy Marketing only works with one orthodontist in a given market.

Dr. Dustin Burleson
Burleson Orthodontics

REALITY OR BS?

IS IT REALLY POSSIBLE TO BOOK YOURSELF SOLID?

> *"I have missed more than 9,000 shots in my career. I have lost almost 300 games. Twenty-six times, I've been trusted to take the game winning shot and missed. I've failed over and over and over again in my life. And that is why I succeed."* **Michael Jordan**

Why is it that the best orthodontists in the world in terms of the treatment they provide don't have the largest and best practices?

Why is it that some orthodontists have bigger practices than others?

How is it that two orthodontists have gone to the same school, yet one of them is earning three times more than the other?

- Each works hard.
- Each has a beautiful office.

- Each has a great staff.
- Each uses the best, most advanced techniques.

And yet one of them has more openings than booked appointments.

- He goes to bed at night wondering how he'll make payroll.
- He's spends money on marketing, but nothing seems to work.
- He worries the new orthodontist who just moved into town will draw away his patients. There's not enough business for all the orthodontists in town already; now things will probably get tighter.
- Will he still have a practice in one, five or ten years?

If you can relate at all, then be thankful you got a copy of this book before it was too late.

OR perhaps you already have the largest orthodontic practice in town, but you still want to help more patients. You, too, will be thankful you are reading this book.

Regardless of your current situation, let's get one thing straight:

It's not your fault!

You went to school to become the best orthodontist possible, not to become a marketing guru.

I've written this book just for you, simple and in terms you'll easily understand.

Think of it as a private consultation with me, during which I'll pull back the curtain and share with you EXACTLY what you've been doing wrong – and, more importantly, how to fix it and fix it FAST.

You hold in your hands what I sincerely hope is the most truthful, blunt, straightforward, non-sugarcoated, no-holds-barred book ever written on marketing and systematizing for orthodontists.

A system to automatically fill your waiting room.

To book more appointments for you than you can handle.

No, I'm not an orthodontist.

But what I am is

- An expert in getting the phone to ring and consultations to be made.

- An expert on fairly and ethically grabbing patients from your competition and helping you treat more patients.

- An expert on analyzing what you do better than your competition and turning that into a magic money faucet that you can turn on at will, watching it pour out as much money as you want.

- An expert on helping you automatically attract more new patients who are searching for an orthodontist right in your local market even while you sleep, providing you time to spend with family, take that well-deserved vacation or properly fund your retirement.

- An expert at squeezing every last penny out of any marketing dollar you invest. In fact, it's not unheard of my 3-step system to give you back five or more dollars for every dollar you spend.
- An expert at truly holding your marketing dollars accountable and helping you track accurate return on investment.
- An expert at positioning you to be THE ONLY treatment option in the minds of the potential patients in your market.

The "Walk-Over-Glass" Philosophy

At a conference recently, one of our clients came up to me and shared with me that he genuinely believed that my team and me would literally walk over glass to help him get the biggest return on his marketing dollar investment.

He's right. We would. I have injected this philosophy into our culture at Jimmy Marketing. We fight like hell and do everything we can to see our clients succeed and dominate their market.

As W. Clement Stone said in the 1930s, small hinges move big doors.

We are always looking for those small tweaks – small hinges that can make a massive difference in your practice.

You see personally, I've been doing this since 1997. Making mistakes, investing hundreds of thousands of dollars, and testing, testing, testing to see what works and what doesn't work. Since 2014, we have been helping orthodontists specifically by implementing our proven 3-step system

No theory.

Just real-world results.

Now, not every orthodontist gets results like Dr. Burleson right away. Sometimes we have to tweak and test more, but typically we get profitable results right from the start.

I've spent more time in the marketing classroom of hard knocks than you did in dental school.

I don't believe in confusing fantasy with "accurate thinking." I believe in measuring every marketing dollar spent and holding it 100 percent accountable to bring a stream (not just a trickle) of money flowing in.

It's why we offer multiple money-back guarantee results for our clients.

This Is A "Go-For-The-Jugular" Book

I've written this book as a private consultation with me – talking straight with you – like you were paying me a five-figure consulting fee and getting all the secrets out of me as if the success of your practice depended on it (which it very well could).

I'm sick and tired of seeing orthodontist after orthodontist get ripped off by these smooth-talking, template-pushing salesmen.

Just reading and putting into practice what I share in this book may very well change your practice.

I seriously thought about putting a price of $1,000 on this book — which would have been cheap for what I'm about to share with you— so you'd truly realize its value.

I don't want this to be one of those books you get and put it on the shelf and never read. Each and every secret I share with you has been carefully tested and retested for results.

Its primary job is to show you how to book yourself solid. Faster than you ever believed possible.

- This book is about getting rich.
- It's about automating your marketing so you have more time off and peace of mind.
- It's about being able to sleep at night knowing (not just guessing) how many calls from prospective patients you'll get in the next day, week, or month.
- It's all about working the number of hours you want to work and still having a great life.

If that offends you, please stop reading.

This book is not for you.

Competition is getting tougher every day and to succeed you have to have the right mindset. The "hope" method of practice management (hope the phone will ring and you'll get new patients coming in for a free consult) doesn't work.

Yellow pages are dead.

Newspapers are dead.

Template websites are dead.

Corporate dentistry is attempting to take over the industry.

Smile Direct Club and other at-home treatment solutions are becoming more and more popular.

You can't rely solely on referrals from dentists as most are competing against you.

Even referrals from other patients are going online and researching you and your practice BEFORE they even call you.

The world is changing – rapidly.

Save us both a lot of time and wasted energy and close this book up if you don't have an open mind to at least consider thinking about the secrets I'm going to share with you.

No Fantasy
Sold As Reality

But if you have even the smallest amount of curiosity – if I can actually show you how to do what I've done with countless orthodontists – then keep reading.

I hope you profit greatly from our relationship, and as always, I wish you the best of success.

I welcome your comments, thoughts, questions, feedback. You can communicate with myself or a Jimmy Marketing team member by contacting us online through our website at https://www.JimmyMarketing.com or calling us at 860.442.9999.

Jimmy Nicholas
Author, Speaker, Agency Owner, Consultant
and Daddy of little Carter

P.S. Go to page 135 for details on a special offer
because you are reading this book.

CHAPTER ONE

WHO AM I AND WHY SHOULD YOU LISTEN TO ME?

My name is Jimmy Nicholas. My beautiful wife, Jennifer, and I are parents of the cutest little boy, Carter.

Since a young child, I've always been very entrepreneurial. If I wasn't shoveling snow or cutting grass, I was selling and making a profit on baseball cards. Growing up I had a great childhood. My parents supported and encouraged my entrepreneurial spirit.

My parents didn't argue much, but when they did, I noticed it seemed to usually be about money. My mom was a teacher and my dad delivered oil.

We had a nice home and my parents sacrificed so much for my own success. I realized their limited budgets from their jobs oftentimes made finances tight.

In my mind JOB equaled **J**ust **O**ver **B**roke. I never wanted to live like that.

So at age 15, I decided I needed to learn how to make money on demand. I realized learning how to market would be the skill that if I could master it, would provide financial freedom. I read every book I could get my hands on about sales and marketing.

It was 1997 and this thing called The Internet had just been starting out. There were these virtual places I could visit all around the world called "websites."

It fascinated me.

I saw the potential in those websites for businesses. On my desk was a telephone book I had been using to call my lawn service clients. It was that day I went from working with individuals to working with businesses.

I opened the yellow pages and began to call.

Business after business turned me down as I tried to explain what a website was and that I could create one for them. (I was going to have to do some quick learning how to do it, but it was a challenge I was excited about.)

Finally – after about 250 calls – a local business said "Yes, come and talk to me about it right now."

Remember, I was 15.

I couldn't drive and the store was too far for me to walk or ride my bike.

Fortunately, my mom was home and she happily agreed to drive me to the appointment and wait for me.

Two hours later, with a check from my first client, and I was in the website and hosting business, a business which I continued all through high school and college.

In 2005, while my classmates from Bryant University were interviewing for their first jobs, I was making plans to expand my website business by offering more services to my clients.

I also wanted to get out of the hosting part of the business which turned into a commodity. I wanted to create the sites but let someone else worry about hackers, uptime and storage.

I wanted to help our clients in bigger ways by providing extremely profitable marketing solutions.

College was great for the basics, but I knew there was a whole lot more to learn about this marketing stuff than I knew at that time.

So I began to seek out the best of the best marketers in the world to learn from them.

I invested hundreds of thousands of dollars and at one point I was even a quarter million dollars in debt paying for this post-college, real-world education. I never thought of it as an expense. It was an investment in my future – a future where I wouldn't be working in one of those J.O.B.s.

I was a sponge and wanted to learn as much as I could as quickly as I could. I put conferences, training and private meetings on my credit card knowing that someday it would pay off. Ultimately, this specialized knowledge would help my company get much better results for our clients.

Slowly but surely it did.

I realized the websites I had built for clients were good, but what they said and how they said it was the real key to opening the money-making vault for our clients.

My main marketing mentor, Dan Kennedy, used the term "magnetic marketing." He described how if you match the message with the market using the right media, you would have a golden key.

Me with my marketing mentor, Dan Kennedy.

I knew that websites — albeit combined with more traditional offline marketing media like direct mail — were a must media.

He also said that the riches were in the niches.

Specialists make more money than generalists.

If I was to become a specialist, I needed to focus on one or two specific industries and learn their languages (the messages) then create a money-making machine for them unlike any other website companies could do.

My first niche was podiatrists.

I worked with them for several years and for many I succeeded in tripling the amount of leads they were getting from the web. We still work with all our podiatric clients and continue to get them even more leads from the web.

In 2013, I met an orthodontist, Dr. Dustin Burleson.

Dr. Burleson and I were actually competing in 2013 for the coveted titled of "Marketer of the Year" at the 1,000-person marketing super conference Dan Kennedy holds every year. There were four of us chosen that year out of 30,000 marketers world-wide who follow Dan's marketing advice to compete.

The stakes were high.

The competition, fierce.

In the end, I won and was celebrated as the best direct-response marketer world-wide.

Little did I realize that day would change the course of my marketing company.

A week after I got home I received a hand-written note from Dr. Burleson congratulating me on my win. I was blown away. For the next year and a half, our paths crossed in various high-level marketing meetings. During one dinner, I was sharing how I was working with podiatrists who were tripling the amount of leads they were attracting from the web after having us implement my 3-step system.

Dr. Burleson was impressed and asked if I thought it could work with orthodontists.

I wasn't sure, but I told him we could test it and find out.

He referred me to one of his coaching clients. Dr. Burleson coaches and consults over 1,900 orthodontists in over 23 countries. We implemented my 3-step system, and he went from virtually ZERO online leads to 19 leads in 45 days with 14 of those leads converting into appointments and many ultimately becoming patients.

Burleson was convinced and hired us to implement the same 3-step system for his practice.

Today, I lead a team of marketing specialists at Jimmy Marketing where we are blessed to help hundreds of orthodontists predictably attract more new patients from the web.

I also get to speak to doctors and orthodontists all over the world.

Dr. Burleson and Jimmy Marketing has teamed up very well. While he coaches on their operations, offline marketing and how to improve the overall patient experience, my team helps with their online marketing by ...

- Helping them identify their unique marketing messages.
- Redesigning their websites from a typical brochure based website into an automatic patient generating machine.
- Installing a dynamic call tracking system to see who's calling and which traffic source those new patient phone calls are coming from.
- Optimizing and sending people who are actively looking for an orthodontist to their website.
- Listening to incoming calls to see which ones turn into new patients so we know what traffic sources are working profitably.
- Constantly testing, tweaking and monitoring their ads.

In short, our team helps the orthodontist attract more ideal prospects into the practice and Dr. Burleson helps orthodontists turn those prospects into paying patients.

The Results:

As of this printing, most of our orthodontists are averaging between 15 to 150 new patient leads a month with 40 percent to 90 percent turning into patients from web marketing. Our client retention rate has been over 93% for years without making our clients sign any contracts and letting them be month-to-month with our services.

CHAPTER TWO

HARSH REALITY – WHAT THIS BOOK IS NOT ABOUT

I think it's important to take a few minutes and talk about what this book is NOT about – to get some of your fears, skepticism and doubts out of the way, to set your mind at ease so you open your mind to what I have to share with you.

First, let's get something straight right out of the gate: **This book is not for every orthodontist**. Some will want to grow their practice and help as many patients in their marketplace as possible; some will want to coast as is.

This is NOT a book for orthodontists who are happy with the number of patients they're currently attracting into their practice.

If you're happy, then don't change a thing in your practice. Congratulations! This book is for those orthodontists who want to grow their practice and have the mindset to invest and re-invest into marketing as long as it is profitable marketing. Working with Dr. Burleson, we've even had some mutual clients more than double their practice in just one year.

This is NOT a book for orthodontists who don't want to invest in marketing or have no money to invest in their marketing.

Budgets will vary from a few thousand to up to fifteen thousand per month or even more. The speed and end goal will dictate the amount invested. The clients who are investing the most amount of money are in markets where they can buy significant amounts of traffic. Because we are tracking every traffic source and hold their marketing dollars accountable, the more money invested into marketing, the more new patients the practice profitably helps.

Typically, our clients start with a smaller testing budget, and we look for pockets of profit within campaigns. Once we know which ads are profitable then we scale the campaigns to ensure profitability.

Now, if you don't have any marketing budget or simply don't want to invest in your marketing, then this book is not for you. We only work with orthodontists who are looking to take their practices and their lives to the next level. They're focused. Obviously, to implement our 3-step system requires a marketing budget.

This is NOT a book for orthodontists who have "heard it all," "tried it all" and won't open their minds to the possibilities of changes making a huge difference in their practices.

An elephant can lift more than a ton with its trunk, but if you see an elephant in a circus, it is tied by a very thin rope that could easily break. When it was young, the elephant was tied by a very heavy chain to a big, immovable stake. It tried and tried to break free but couldn't. Soon it stopped trying and accepted its fate.

Too many orthodontists are like this elephant. They've tried and tried other marketing methods, spent a lot of money doing so. And nothing worked, or if it did, it did not work very well. They are stuck within their own limitations, manufactured by their own beliefs and experiences. They're not open to the possibility that something really can work and that I really can do what I say I can do. This book is not for those orthodontists.

This is NOT a book for orthodontists who cannot commit a couple of hours a month to their marketing.

While I share all my secrets to doubling — and sometimes tripling or even more — your online leads, it does require some time to implement what I'm about to share with you. If you hire the Jimmy Marketing team to implement this 3-step system, it will require significantly less time than if you tried to implement the 3-step system yourself (to the tune of saving about 1,000 hours per year). When you hire Jimmy Marketing, we simply need a few phone calls of about an hour or less in the first few months and then a call or two per month to discuss results and what we are tweaking for you.

Now that you know a bit about me and who this book is NOT for, let get started with my book yourself solid secrets.

CHAPTER THREE

YOUR MARKETING MINDSET

SECRET #1

Understand People Are Searching For You Online & Your Website Critically Matters

For those of you reading this book who aren't currently attracting patients from the web you may not believe that prospective patients or moms of prospective patients would search online for their orthodontist and call you.

For many of you reading this book, you may find it hard to believe that people today go online, they search for an orthodontist, then based on the website that they find, they either call or don't call you. Literally, without you doing anything but showing up online and having the right website, you can get hot potential patients who are interested in braces or Invisalign for themselves or for their children literally calling you all day long.

It's especially mind-boggling for those of you who've relied on just building your practice without any advertising or marketing and you're just growing based on referrals. Well, remember how I said the marketplace has changed considerably? People aren't choosing you as their orthodontist because you went to the best school or you have more years of schooling than a dentist. They're choosing you based on your website and the faster you can grasp this concept, the faster you can grow your practice.

Look, I'm being harsh and blunt here because I have to. I want to help you help more patients, so that being said, I'm going to share with you a transcript of a clip from one of our clients for an actual patient phone call. Listen to what she says.

Vicky: Hi, it's Vicky speaking, how may I help you?

Mom: Hi, I have a question. My daughter went to the dentist yesterday and they wanted her to get four extractions, for her wisdom teeth. I called them to see about getting an appointment but they asked me who was my … or who we were going to be going to for her braces.

Vicky: Okay.

Mom: I've been doing my research. This has been a nightmare, I swear, and I ran across your website and it was the most easiest website I have been on within the past few days. So I am giving you guys a call to see when can I start up this initial ...

Vicky: Evaluation. Yes, Ma'am. Well, first of all, thank you so much for saying that. We do appreciate it. We actually just revamped the website.

Mom: Oh, did you really?

Vicky: So, that's some great feedback. I will definitely let the Doctor know.

So because this orthodontist, again who happens to be one of our clients, has a great website that is easy to use, the caller subconsciously thinks he must be a better orthodontist than the other orthodontists in town, because his website, and I quote, "Was the most easiest website I have been on in the past few days, so I'm giving you guys a call."

Notice, she didn't say because he is this great orthodontist who went to some Ivy-League school and then additional schooling, but because our client made the decision, to invest in their web presence by hiring us, this mom and the many other moms coming to their website subconsciously think that this orthodontist with the great website has to be the best orthodontist for her child.

Today, we are finding even word of mouth referrals from patients and dentists are still going online and they are looking at your website BEFORE they even call your office.

This next clip is from a dad calling into another one of our clients' offices. His daughter's dentist referred our clients and two other orthodontists to the father. Ultimately, he called our client because of the website.

Felice: Felice speaking. How can I help you?

Dad: Yeah, I have a nine-year-old daughter and I just wanted to schedule a no-obligation assessment with the doctor.

Felice: Wonderful. It would be the first time for anybody in your family coming in?

Dad: Yes, that's right.

Felice: Okay, great. Yeah, we can definitely set you up the consultation. It's totally free and it's an hour long, and it can go to an hour and a half if you decide you wanted to stay and get started, but let's get some information in the system first.

Dad: Okay, sure.

Felice: Who recommended you to us, how did you ...

Dad: Actually, we go to doctor ... and he's our dentist. [Practice Name] Orthodontics was one of the cards he gave us, and actually, I did look at your website and I must say it's a very impressive website.

Felice: Oh, thank you so much.

Dad: Not just in terms of how good the website is, the technology behind it, but in terms of the ...It just, it gives a person coming to it for the first time or looking to see orthodontics, it makes a person feel good and it's very impressive, I must say.

Felice: Oh, thank you so much. We really appreciate that. We worked really hard getting that website together with a team.

Dad: Yeah. Yeah, that's one thing. Even the content behind it, right? It gives you all the information and that free download that you had of what you should be looking for. I think that's very good.

Felice: Thank you.

Dad: It's good without being crass.

Felice: Right. I know, sometimes either you get too much information or too little, or too flashy.

Dad: I mean, and then sometimes you can just ... Yeah, you just see through the marketing hype, but that's exactly what it wasn't. Just the right amount of everything, so it was a job well done.

My goal for sharing those two clips with you is for you to truly believe that web marketing is important, and even more important than that, it's that the right web marketing is most critical for your success.

Would you want more calls coming into your practice like the two I shared?

Well, because you are reading this book you are most likely looking to grow your practice and help more patients, I would venture to say that the answer is yes.

So being your website is the most critical component and foundation to all of your marketing, in the next chapter I will share with you how to get your website right.

CHAPTER FOUR

YOUR WEBSITE

SECRET #2

Set Up Your Foundation To Your Profitable Marketing System

Dr. Smith (not his real name) was like so many other orthodontists I speak with. He had paid a website design firm to have his website designed (multiple times) – paying good money each time.

He liked the websites they'd designed for others and knew he wanted to attract more patients and increase his production. He knew a website was important, so he had hired them.

He didn't quite know what to expect but was surprised when they asked him to give them what he wanted to say on the site.

He wasn't sure.

He wasn't that great of a writer.

He thought that they would write all the content, so when they didn't, he reluctantly turned over that part to a gal in his office. She spent hours working on the project and finally the website was up and live.

He was confident he was the best orthodontist in his market, so he was hopeful the new site would increase his practice. Many of his patients had told him he was the best-kept secret and they were so glad they found him.

Life was going to be good now.
The phone was going to ring.
The schedule was going to be filled.

The key foundation to any marketing these days is your website – whether it's referrals, online, newspaper, radio, billboards, direct mail, you name it. Today, just about every prospect checks out your website before making a decision to even call you. And many times from a mobile device.

Even if their friends recommend you or their dentist refers them to you, they will still go to your site to check you out first.

Your job is to speak directly to the prospect most likely to buy, perfectly qualified to buy, and reach out through your website to figuratively grab him or her to call and make an appointment for a consultation. It's no small task.

Reality sets in for Dr. Smith.

Things didn't quite work out the way he hoped they would.

The phone didn't ring any more than before. His schedule was still wide open. He even tried Google Ad Words, spots on the local TV station, ads in the newspaper. He tried a lot of things — and nothing really worked. He was frustrated and didn't know what to do.

Dr. Smith heard about me through another orthodontist. He listened with envy as the other orthodontist told him the results she was getting from her Jimmy Marketing website and ongoing marketing.

"What the heck?" he thought. "I'll call Jimmy Marketing and see what they have to say. Maybe they could just fine-tune my current site and then the calls would finally start coming in."

His first telephone call with Darren Mason, our top marketing advisor...

When Darren asked how many patients came from his site, he couldn't tell him.

When Darren asked how much was his return on the investment he made, he couldn't tell him.

When Darren asked how much his practice had grown after the website redesign, he said it hadn't.

We have heard that same story time after time. What he'd paid for was a poorly converting "brochure" website with no ongoing strategy to attract potential new patients to the site.

It happens in every industry and it happens all of the time.

It's because the companies designing websites are tech heads – not marketers who hold every dollar spent accountable to bring more money back into the practice.

In fact, when Darren looked at the website it was cluttered, disorganized and confusing. While it looked good with big pictures, there was no messaging or reasons to call Dr. Smith instead of any other orthodontist.

But Dr. Smith was already ahead of the game. He knew what he didn't know and was still willing to open his mind to listen to possibilities.

Dr. Smith was willing to be coachable.

He had the right mindset to make a change – even if it was a small one to start with.

If he kept doing what he'd always been doing, he probably would stay in the same place. With competition always trying to take away business, chances are he wouldn't grow — and might very well see his profits dwindle more. Who knows if he'd still be in business in five years unless something changed.

This is not what he'd signed up for when he went to orthodontic school.

As hard as it was to put aside the thought of the money he'd just spent over the past 6-12 months, he decided to do just that and listen.

SECRET #3

Start First With A Unique Message - The Logo Test

I want you to look at your website and do "The Logo Test." The Logo Test is simple, if you took off your logo and replaced it with a competitor's logo, would the information on the site basically still hold true? If the answer is "Yes, it could be anyone's site," then you basically have a typical brochure site with no differentiation.

There's no compelling reason for that mom to pick up the phone and call you. She'll check all the local orthodontic sites looking for a reason to call one. She could as easily throw a dart because no one particular orthodontist is standing out as the logical and clear choice.

You must use your unique message to magnetically draw her in.

Contrast that to a website that has a carefully crafted message that speaks directly to her. It's almost as if you know the conversation happening inside her head. She may not realize it, but it is magnetically attracting her to you and you alone. You stand out from all the other orthodontic sites. You catch her attention. She has to call.

Every client we work with begins with our unique discovery process which starts with us giving you an asset gathering checklist. Our team also performs competitive and keyword research to know what you are up against in your market. Then, you have a simple phone call with our Website Marketing Specialist. On that call, we ask you a series of questions to help uncover how you are unique and different. Sometimes we help you make some tweaks and innovations in your practice so moms and potential patients will be magnetically attracted to calling your practice. We also help leverage things you are most likely not even thinking about leveraging in your marketing right now. We build your entire marketing message around your uniqueness.

Apples to oranges.

I like to say it's an apples-to-oranges comparison.

When your competition has a brochure site that says the same thing as everyone else, it becomes a game of chance who they'll call.

They're all selling "apples."

But if you help your prospect buy "oranges," you change the game.

Notice the difference. People don't want to be sold. They want to buy. So your job is to help them buy. And if you differentiate yourself – do a great job at branding – they're not buying apples; they realize what they really want is oranges.

It's a subtle difference and one that is a total game changer. You're the expert. And when you offer "oranges" for them to buy (which is what they really need), price resistance goes down. I've seen one orthodontist who originally was charging $4,300 for an average case, but when he understood this principle and changed one simple thing, he was able to charge $7,500 for basically the same treatment. He was offering something no one else in his area offered. He was unique and was able to explain that uniqueness.

Here's some examples from some of our real clients. Remember: these are just a few examples of the hundreds we have done. Figure out your own uniqueness and build your marketing around it or go to page 135 to take advantage of the special offer for readers of this book so we can personally help you.

Unique messaging examples:
- Worry-free treatment
- Insurance and easy payment plans available
- No money down starts
- Braces without missing work or school
- Transform your smile up to 50% faster
- Correct previous treatment in as little as five weeks
- Family discounts available
- Lifetime guarantee
- Same-day appointments
- Same-day braces
- Many options with even braces behind your teeth
- Award-winning
- Top rated

Again, so we can personally guide you with your own unique message to help you magnetically attract patients into your practice, turn to page 135 to take advantage of the special offer to readers of this book only.

SECRET #4

What Your Website Shouldn't Have

I have nine don'ts that if you have on your site they will absolutely kill response. If you learn nothing else from this book, pay very, very close attention to these.

- DON'T list just services and solutions.

    A lot of orthodontic practices out there just list different services and solutions. And it's like a laundry list of things that you do. You understand what all these different things mean. But the average person who isn't an orthodontist is not going to understand what the list of different services and solutions can do for them in terms of a transformational result.

    People are looking for the result – not a bunch of technical terms.

- DON'T use "Welcome to …" as a headline or lead in on your website. Somewhere someone must have written a website manual that says all sites must start that way because there are so many that do. You're wasting valuable online real estate. Hard-hitting, direct and laser-focused benefit copy will always convert better than the bland, watered-down, just-like-everyone-else "Welcome to…."

- DON'T use a standard template website. Saving money by using an off-the-shelf template is not wise. There's minimal return on that investment when a custom, direct-response, message-driven site can always pay for itself and more.

- DON'T put your social media icons at the top of your site. I'm sure many would argue with me on this one, but remember, I test everything. And I don't want that person who found your site to be distracted by their Facebook, Pinterest, Instagram, Twitter or whatever is the current rage. We have very few precious seconds to catch their attention and get them convinced to pick up the phone and call your office. I don't want to compete with Aunt Millie's pie picture she just posted. You can put your social media icons in the footer of your website.

- DON'T talk to just one audience. You may be tempted to focus your website on just moms of kids and ignore entirely the 20-33-year-old or even the 50-65-year-old markets. If they don't feel you have a solution for them, they'll go elsewhere.

- DON'T have multiple navigations on your website. You should only have one clean horizontal navigation on your website. I've seen websites with two horizontal navigations and a left-side navigation. I have my own thoughts about why a single horizontal navigation works best, but remember, I test everything. When we add code on a website to watch what people do, hands down a simple horizontal navigation results in the website visitor staying longer and reading more. I don't have to understand the underlying psychology of "why" this is. I just accept it is and make that a standard on all sites we design.

- DON'T put a digital report you've written behind an email opt-in form. Putting reports behind an opt-in used to work, but not as much anymore.

  But for most, people are wise to the fact their email will go into an email drip sequence and they already get too much "junk" email. They don't want more. They simply want the information. So give it to them. You want an automatic patient attraction system, not put road blocks in front of them. We have found with our clients that they receive five times more calls from prospects if they can simply read the report and not have to give their name and email. The key is that the report is written in a way to move the prospect to the next step and book their initial consultation.

- DON'T have a different website for each location if all your locations are within the same state. You may not have multiple locations. But if you do and they are all within the same state, DO NOT create a site for each one. Maintaining multiple sites can be a slippery slope to frustration. It can be confusing for the prospect and a nightmare for your staff to maintain. There's simply no need to do it. Now, if you have practices in multiple states, each state should have its own website. You will find your sites should rank higher on Google.

- DON'T have multiple phone numbers listed in the upper right. What should happen, however, is that you have a way to easily transfer calls to each location. One phone number in the upper right on the website is ideal. The easier you make it for people to contact you, the easier you can make it for them to do business with you.

Now on to the dos.

SECRET #5

Guarantee Your Services

We talk to orthodontists all the time who do not have a guarantee. Yet they stand behind their work. They just don't tell anyone they do, and certainly they're not putting it on their website or in their marketing.

Let me ask you a question.

What would it cost you if you had a patient come back to see you in three or four years and you needed to put braces back on? Or tweak something with a retainer?

How many patients do you think would be in that situation?

If you said "not many," you're right!

The benefit to have a lifetime guarantee would far outweigh the cost.

Never underestimate the power of a guarantee.

It is my conviction and advice that if you feel you cannot guarantee your services, you need to reinvent your practice until you can.

It also matters how the guarantee is worded. "Satisfaction guaranteed or your money back," is ok, and any guarantee is better than none. "Unconditional, lifetime guarantee," is a much more powerful statement.

Look at your competition.

Check out their websites.

Do any of them have such a strong guarantee?

What if the patient who chooses you because of your guarantee and, in a worst case scenario, exercises the guarantee? And particularly if the problem was their fault because they didn't wear their retainer? The little amount of cost and time for you to help them will be worth the investment of them telling their friends about how you stood behind your guarantee.

I realize implementing a guarantee may be something you don't want to do right now, and that is fine. However, keep in mind, all of our clients who have implemented a guarantee have seen a significant increase in their bottom line.

SECRET #6

Brand Everything In Your Practice

- Brand your guarantee.
- Brand your consultation.
- Brand your services.

It goes back to the apples-to-oranges comparison. When you brand the solutions your practice offers, no one can compare you on price.

For example, instead of just calling it a lifetime guarantee, Dr. Burleson calls it The Burleson Lifetime Guarantee.

The Burleson Lifetime Guarantee

At Burleson Orthodontics, we stand behind our treatment for you or your children. During your initial exam and complimentary consultation, ask for more details on the "Burleson 100% Lifetime Guarantee."

This guarantee is just one of the reasons why Burleson is different. At Burleson Orthodontics, we offer a variety of treatment options for straight teeth in our Kansas City, Liberty, Raymore, and Excelsior Springs, MO, orthodontic offices.

Start here to see if Burleson Orthodontics is right for you.

Every orthodontist with a template, brochure-based website has a complimentary consultation. To set you apart, create a special consultation "package" and give it a name. Brand it.

For example, here's Dr. Burleson's description of his complimentary exam, with an easy call to action button: Make Appointment.

Receive Your Complimentary Burleson Orthodontics Exam, Consultation, Digital X-Rays ($249 Value)

Also Receive From Dr. Burleson:
• Free Best-Selling Book
• Free DVD Resource Guide
• And More!

MAKE APPOINTMENT

Chances are you have several advanced techniques and services you offer patients that other orthodontists in your area may or may not offer. Each of these techniques has a manufacturer, equipment and brand behind them. But I teach my clients NOT to publicize those brand names. Instead, give it a name that shows a benefit and is special to you by using your name. For example, if you offer Propel or Acceledent, instead of mentioning their name, you should say Save up to ½ the treatment time with your practice name instead of with Acceledent.

SECRET #7

Speak To Your Audience

Brochure sites try to be a one-size-fits-all. "Welcome to …" blah, blah, blah.

Not a Jimmy Marketing website.

We want that prospect who's found you to read exactly what he or she is looking for so your website speaks directly to their needs.

So you always want to have a section that says: You are here because (and the because should be specific to your practice). Here are a few examples that have worked successfully.

- You want to learn about braces for your child.
- You want to learn about braces for yourself.

- You or your child have jaw pain and migraines.
- You were referred to (your practice name).
- You want a second opinion.
- You want to learn more about Invisalign.

Having a "you are here because" section helps turn your website into a tool that assists your sales process and helps you build bonding, rapport and trust instantly because your ideal audience will feel like they are in the right place. The more trust you can build automatically on your website, the more yeses you will receive.

With marketing it's the simple – but often overlooked – things that can make the difference of adding an additional $100,000 to your monthly bottom line and keeping you booked solid.

SECRET #8

Utilize Free Reports

A certain percentage of the prospects coming to your site will be readers. They want to digest all the information before making a decision of whether they should call or not call you for the initial consultation. You need to have more information for that person to want to call you. A .pdf document that someone can download and read is perfect for the thorough reader.

Not every person will download the report and read it. But a certain number will. You need to have the report to serve the audience that does want to read more and provide the information they are craving.

Two special reports that work well for our orthodontic clients are "The Top 10 things to Know Before Choosing Your Orthodontist" and "Does Your Child Really Need Braces?" with a download now button to instantly read the free report.

No email required. The reason why is simple. When the report is designed and the messaging is crafted in a way to position you as the logical AND only choice for treatment, you do not want to put up a barrier of asking for their email address to read the report. The report assists your sales process, so make it easy for people to access the report.

Of course in the special report you need to be sure you have a call to action to call you and make an appointment for a free consultation – that initial assessment that you have developed and branded for your practice.

SECRET #9

Leverage 5-Star Reviews

Who wants to go to the orthodontist who is speaking their language, has a strong guarantee, has an easy to navigate website AND has 5-star reviews?

If there's one thing that I see so many orthodontists ignore is properly leveraging their reviews. Some will have reviews on Google, Yelp, etc., but most aren't replicating those reviews on to their website. Additionally, many aren't using the logo of the review website with 5-stars to help build trust and credibility.

It's 1,000 times more important what your patients say about you than what you say about yourself. Creating a culture of "WOW" is the first step to getting 5-star reviews. Once you have reviews, leverage them onto your website as well.

Google, Yelp, HealthGrades, Angie's List, Yellow Pages – there's a lot of places your patients can leave reviews.

Pick out the best ones and replicate them on your site.

NOTE: Reviews are a double-edged sword. Anyone and everyone can leave a review. Someone in your office (or our staff if you're working with us) should always be monitoring reviews and responding to anything negative.

Overwhelmingly positive reviews will outweigh the negative, but never ignore the negative ones. If you happen to receive a negative review, respond publicly and offer to help them offline.

Build And Leverage Credibility With Memberships And Logos

You are most likely a member of the American Association of Orthodontists, potentially the American Dental Association and maybe even more associations and societies. Use all those logos on your site.

Look for opportunities to be interviewed by the media – online, in print, on TV, on radio, anywhere. When you've been interviewed or quoted, you can build credibility by using those logos also on your site.

One organization most orthodontists never even consider is the Better Business Bureau. Yes, I know you have to pay to be a member. Most parents, patients and prospective patients – decision makers – don't' know that. But when you're accredited and graded by them, you can add their logo to your website also.

Combined, all these logos add up to help build more credibility and trust with your website visitors. The more you have, the more overwhelming the evidence that you are the number one choice in the area.

People choose the orthodontist they choose based on trust. This is why referrals are typically easier to say yes to your treatment than someone who comes into your practice who wasn't referred to you. The more trust you can build with your website, the less time you and your team will need to take to build that rapport.

SECRET #11

Leverage Celebrity Opportunities

People love celebrities. They're fascinated with their lives. While it makes no sense, they associate "celebrity" with "credibility and trust," which is why this is one of my secrets to helping you attract more new patients into your practice.

Since you're doing business on a local level, it's relatively easy and inexpensive to use celebrity in your business – and of course – on your website. It might take a bit of imagination, but here's a couple of ideas.

1.   **You can be the celebrity.** Make yourself famous by writing articles, being interviewed on the radio and TV, writing your own book, giving lectures and being active in the community. Press releases sent out on a regular basis can help improve your perceived celebrity status. You could also host your own radio show or TV show online.

I was recently interviewed by Leeza Gibbons (Emmy Award Winner & Form Entertainment Tonight Co-Host), Kevin Harrington (one of the original sharks on ABC's hit show, "Shark Tank") and Jack Canfield (Co-Author of <u>The Chicken Soup for the Soul</u>

book series with over 500 million books sold). Being interviewed as "the expert" gave me celebrity status that I now leverage in our marketing.

Look out for sound bytes in interviews that you can leverage. For example, in the interview with Leeza Gibbons, she said "Jimmy Marketing is America's most trusted marketing team." In the interview with Kevin Harrington, he said, "Jimmy Marketing websites not only look great, but they perform top-notch, especially for doctors." In the interview with Jack Canfield, he said, "Jimmy can take your practice ot the next level." All of these sound bytes we have leveraged on our website, in our print materials, and in our presentations.

And of course, winning Marketer of the Year for the world's largest direct response marketing organization gave me massive celebrity status, which is leverage.

2.   **If any local celebrity comes into your practice, approach him or her about using his or her testimonial on your website.** It's possible there may be a fee required (or maybe you give them free services) to use them as an endorsement, but it will be far less than getting a national celebrity and potentially be even more effective.

It is not at all unusual for people to need to prove that they are making the right decision when choosing an orthodontist. If the local "celebrity" or Mr. or Ms. Celebrity is using your services, people rationalize that there must be something special about you and your services.

One thing to keep in mind: The celebrity you choose must relate to your audience, someone the audience would admire.

SECRET #12

Have Simple Navigation

Confused people don't buy, which is why here at Jimmy Marketing we invest so much time on the navigation and layout of the website. We don't use templates. The location and positioning of all the elements on your website will affect the number of calls you'll receive.

Because we customize every website to the orthodontic practice, we can organize the unique information in a way that makes the most sense to the specific audience of the orthodontist.

Seven of Jimmy Marketing's absolutes:

1. Phone number in the upper right-hand corner.
2. "Request Appointment" button that really stands out in the header.
3. Logo in the upper left, but not so large as to overpower the site.
4. Horizontal navigation bar.
5. Website passes the logo test.
6. Areas for unique messaging tailored to specific audiences

7. Use multiple sections on a website to organize and display information in a clear way.

SECRET #13

Have An Introduction Paragraph Or Letter

Think of your homepage as the welcome mat into your practice. You're talking like you would to a friend or family member. Use conversational language in either a paragraph or letter format. If you choose the letter format, don't forget to add at least one "P.S." It's proven when people read letters, they read the P.S. first. For the P.S. be sure to include your call to action to your branded initial consultation.

Also, be sure to bold the important sentences so it's easy to read, especially for the person who likes to skim text. In Dr. Burleson's case the first sentence in each

paragraph is bolded. You can see his intro paragraph
by visiting:

http://www.BurlesonOrthodontics.com

SECRET #14

Utilize Video

Video also helps build rapport and trust when crafted
with the right messaging. Scripted correctly, prospects
will stay on your site longer because of video. The
longer they stay, the more they are going to feel like
they're starting to build a relationship with you. They
are looking for a reason to trust you. Video helps develop a rapport to give them that reason.

A homepage video should tell them what it's like to
work with you and your staff. How easy is it? How comfortable will they feel? Video allows you to show your
prospects exactly how you look, sound and act. You can
convey personality. Are you young and fun? Bold and as-
sertive? Gentle and caring? Kind and careful?

Knowing your unique message for your website will
direct how you script a video.

Be sure to keep testimonial and video releases on
file if you are using patients in your videos.

SECRET #15

Use Your Own Patient Photos

Studies have proven that actual patient photos have a better chance of engaging your visitors on your website compared to using stock photography. When you use stock photos, there is not as much engagement. You also run the risk of your competitor(s) using the same photo. While it's tempting to use stock photography because it is quicker and usually less expensive, don't use stock photography unless you don't have any other alternative.

Using real photos also helps brand your practice. Before/after photos of real patients also show visual proof of your services. It's best to spend some time with a professional photographer to learn how to take the best photos. Lighting, backgrounds, cameras can all make a difference in the final photos. Great pictures translate to money in the bank because professional photos automatically build more trust.

CHAPTER FIVE

TURBO-CHARGING YOUR RESULTS – ATTRACT MORE OF YOUR IDEAL PROSPECTS TO YOUR WEBSITE

Once you have your website fine-tuned and dialed in to convert prospects into patients, it's time to put your online marketing into overdrive. That means you must invest some money – usually a couple to a few thousand per month – to drive people to your site (depending on if you want to put a toe into the water or jump all in). Our clients typically start with a smaller testing budget. Once a traffic source has proven itself to be profitable, then you should scale and increase the marketing budget.

Since we work with orthodontists in different markets, we tend to have a head start as to what works and what doesn't work. Because of our access to so much historical data and our winning ad bank, we are typically able to shortcut our client's path to success.

SECRET #16

Spy On Your Competition Before Launching Any Marketing Campaigns

With the data that is available today, you really should see what your competition locally as well as national competitors are doing when it comes to advertising online. Keep in mind, while Invsalign is most likely a partner to you, they are also competing for advertising space on Google and other searching engines which will drive your costs up; however, they do have millions of dollars invested in research and testing, so you definitely want to pay attention to how they are advertising.

You can do a free Google search and see what they are saying in their ads, as well as where the ads go. At Jimmy Marketing, we also use paid tools such as iSpionage which will tell us which ads they have been running longer and most likely how much they are investing online as well as the cost for each ad. You can also get similar information on your local competitors using tools like this.

By arming yourself with this information you are now aware of what you are up against and how you must set yourself apart so you are different than your competition. This information should help you invest less money on your marketing.

SECRET #17

Take Advantage Of Your Lowest Hanging Fruit With Search Engine Marketing

The lowest hanging fruit tends to be Google, Yahoo and Bing search traffic for both free and paid listings on these search engines. When people are searching for an orthodontist, Invisalign, braces or other treatment solutions you offer, you want to ensure you are visible on these search engines in your market.

You should be using PPC and SEO to take up multiple listings on the first page of Google.

Once you have bought all of the search traffic you can buy in your market and you have maximized your SEO visibility, then you should expand your advertising to other traffic sources.

I should also mention that creating things on your website to naturally get ranked on Google for organic search is great tactic to help with your search engine optimization.

SEO is not something to ignore in your practice. Being it changes constantly, I did not include it as its own secret. However, you definitely want to work with someone you trust to manage your own SEO because we typically find our lowest cost per lead for our clients to be from SEO.

SECRET #18

Have An Omnipresent Feel With Retargeting

With retargeting typically only costing between $25 and $50 per week, I am surprised many orthodontists are still not leveraging it within their web marketing.

For those of you reading who don't know what retargeting is, it's a simple technology that allows you to advertise all over the Internet for pennies to people who have been to your website.

Ever been on Amazon or another website looking at a product, and then you see that same product all over the Internet until you ultimately buy it? That is retargeting and you should definitely be using it to create top of mind awareness to the hottest prospects, those who have been to your website.

Think of the power of advertising on Time, CBS, MSN or even your local newspaper. Advertising on these websites directly would typically cost thousands of dollars per month, but with retargeting you can be on those sites for pennies.

Additionally, there is just as much value showing up and advertising on a mom's favorite blog. You build trust and rapport instantly as you are in an environment where she is extremely comfortable.

SECRET #19

Circumvent Google With Facebook Advertising

Have you heard, the right message in front of the right audience at the right time is a winning marketing formula.

With Facebook you can laser target your audience. In fact, you can upload the email addresses and phone numbers of your patient list to Facebook and Facebook will go and find your patients on Facebook. On average a third to half of the people on your patient list are on Facebook. Then, with a click of a button, you can clone your audience and Facebook will go and find similar new people to advertise to.

Facebook is also a great place to test headlines and copy because it is so inexpensive and you get data practically instantly. So before you go and invest thousands of dollars in a direct mail campaign, use Facebook to test the headlines.

Ensure You Have A Solid 5-Star Reputation With Multiple Review Websites

Today, reviews on the public review websites such as Google and Yelp in particular are not "sticking" like they did before. You may find your patients are posting reviews for your practice on Google and Yelp, yet they aren't visible to the public.

Google and Yelp are constantly changing their algorithm that determines which reviews will display publicly and which ones won't.

The best strategy is to have a system in place within your office to help your practice get as many 5-star reviews as possible. There is no shortage of systems available when it comes to increasing your number of online reviews. Most work very well, but all tend to need staff involvement in order to get the most effective results.

We include an automated system, Reviews Accelerator, for our clients which triages the reviews so that any negative ones go directly to the staff to respond and deal with versus having the negative ones be posted on Google or Yelp directly. We can even have the system automatically send the review request.

SECRET #21

Utilize YouTube Videos To Increase Your Visibility Even More

At the time of this printing, the second most commonly used search engine on the Internet is YouTube (behind Google). Did you know that Google owns YouTube? Google will often display YouTube search results within its own search results.

If you have informative videos on YouTube that are properly tagged with the right keywords you will increase your visibility on both YouTube and Google. Having effective video will also allow you to build trust, bonding and rapport with your ideal prospects.

Remember to have a call to action in every video. Some calls to action may be to have people visit your website, click through to a specific blog or page on your website, come into your office, etc.

SECRET #22

Use Citations And Directories To Help Increase Your Rankings With Google

One of the easiest ways to boost your position rankings on Google and other search engines is to ensure your website, address and phone number are properly and accurately listed on directories throughout the Internet.

Each time your physical address and practice's contact information is listed on the Internet that is a citation. Typically, the more citations you have, the more legitimate your practice seems to Google and your website position rankings tend to rise.

Many supposed gurus will tell you that having your link everywhere on the Internet is bad. If your link to your website is on websites which Google considers poor quality or spammy, then that is bad for your Google rankings. However, having your practice listed accurately with links on quality websites to your website is critical to increasing your overall visibility and credibility with Google.

SECRET #23

Distribute Online Press Releases For Increased Credibility And Visibility

In addition to citations, having press releases with links to your website and your practice's contact information will help automatically increase your search engine rankings.

In your press release, make sure you include some of the keyword phrases people are using in the search engines to find the treatment solutions you offer. By incorporating keyword phrases, your press release has a very good chance it will be indexed and displayed within the Google search results. Then, when a potential patient or a mom reads your press release, they will be more apt to trust you. Just like with all of your content that is published off of your website, be sure to have a clear call to action such as directing people to your website for more information or to request their free consultation.

SECRET #24

Utilize Landing Pages Especially With Your Paid Advertising

When a potential patient in your market is searching online for Invsalign, you will most likely find that you will get more people initially clicking on your ads if your ad is about Invisalign versus orthodontics and braces.

Furthermore, if you take that patient to a strategically designed landing page about Invisalign, you will most likely see more people booking their initial appointment with you. From marketing 101, the message must match what the market wants in the right media. You must give the potential patient exactly what they want initially to help you get more yeses to initial appointments. Now the person may or may not be a candidate for Invisalign, but you can determine that during your initial consultation.

Overall, we have found our clients having more success with targeted ads and landing pages instead of just bringing your potential patients to the homepage of your website.

HOLD YOUR MARKETING DOLLARS ACCOUNTABLE

SECRET #25

Use Google Analytics For Online Forms Tracking

Google Analytics gives valuable data beyond just the number of visitors to your website. With Google Analytics you can set up goals to help track where visitors who submit online forms on your website are actually coming from. This helps determine cost per lead by traffic source for the online form submissions.

Additionally, you should pay attention to the trends of a few key metrics from Google Analytics:

- Number of visitors to your website
- Number of pages visited
- Pages per visit

- % of traffic which is mobile vs tablet vs desktop
- Bounce rate

Through proper tracking, you can be more aware of something that's not working. As long as a traffic source is profitable, though, you should continue to utilize as many traffic sources as possible.

Your website person should be able to install some behind-the-scenes code to your site that allows you to track everything!

You must know your numbers, like what ad is resonating with your market, and what ad is not.

If you don't have tracking on your site for every ad you're running, you'll never know where your prospects are coming from.

SECRET #26

Use Dynamic Call Tracking

While many visitors will want to submit an online form or book their initial appointment right on your website, many people will prefer to call your office. At the time of this printing we are seeing about two-thirds of all incoming new patient leads coming in via the phone.

You simply cannot rely solely on Google Analytics to understand which traffic sources are profitable for you and which ones aren't. If you did rely just on

Google Analytics you would be losing out on two-thirds of the data.

You can use a dynamic call tracking system on your website so that the phone number will automatically change throughout your website based on where the visitor has come from. For example, if a visitor comes from a Google Ad they would see X number, if a visitor comes from a Google free listing they would see Y number, if a visitor comes from a Facebook ad they would see Z number and so on. All incoming calls to those numbers should be recorded so that each call can be listened to and categorized properly. Since you would know which phone number is associated with each appropriate traffic source you can now accurately understand which traffic sources are making your phone ring.

SECRET #27

Record & Categorize All Calls For Most Accurate Data

Having dynamic call tracking is a must. Additionally, you want to make sure all of your calls are recorded and listened to. As the calls are listened to, they need to be categorized into:

- New Patient Call That Converted Into An Appointment

- New Patient Call That Did NOT Convert Into An Appointment
- Existing Patient Call
- Non-Lead Call
- Missed/No One Answered Call

Since we listen to every incoming call for the clients we work with, we know that the percentage of calls for our clients that are actual new patient calls varies from 10% to 30%. Therefore, you must know the accuracy of the calls to understand the number of calls coming into the practice which are actual leads.

Many of our competitors will report inflated numbers and not properly report just the lead calls to you. They may be using a call tracking system and just tell you the total number of calls instead of reporting actual leads. When companies just report total number of calls by traffic source and not actual lead calls you are not looking at accurate data.

You should also be aware of them reporting duplicate calls as individual leads. For example, a potential mom calls in for more information. Then, she calls back to schedule the appointment. She calls back a third time to change the appointment time. A majority of our competitors, report this as three leads when in fact it is only one lead.

So in order to ensure you have the right data you must have your calls listened to and properly categorized.

Ideally, you will note the potential patient name so you can track true ROI by traffic source by cross referencing the list of potential patients to ones that sign up for treatment. At Jimmy Marketing, we find the easiest method is to keep a spreadsheet with Patient Names and Traffic Source with a column for you to identify if they started treatment. If you become our client, we also take care of all the listening and categorization of calls for you.

SECRET #28

Look At Your Cost Per Lead Spreadsheet Monthly

You should have a simple spreadsheet where you list the traffic sources down the left-most column and then in the first row you are listing:

- # of New Patient Phone Calls
- # of Lead Calls Converted Into Appointments
- # of Online Form Submissions
- # of Chats (if you are using chats)
- # of Online Appointments Booked (if you are using online appointment booking)
- Total Leads (add up # of New Patient Phone Calls, # of Online Form Submissions, # of Chats and # of Online Appointments)
- Cost (what each traffic source cost)

- Cost Per Lead (Cost / Total Number of Leads for that traffic source)

Below you will see a sample Cost Per Lead Sheet for one of our orthodontists.

Traffic Source	# of Lead Calls	# of Lead Calls Converted	Form Submissions	Total Leads	Cost	Cost Per Lead	Clicks	CPC	Notes
Jimmy Marketing/SEO	68	56	24	92	$3,000.00	$ 32.61			
Google Adwords	23	16	6	29	$4,201.60	$ 144.88	687	$6.12	
Yahoo/Bing PPC			2	2	$ 250.08	$ 125.04	70	$3.57	
Facebook/ Instagram			8	8	$ 396.40	$ 49.55			6 referrals commented on the ad
Retargeting					$ 95.65				
Total	91	72	40	131	$7,943.73	$ 60.64			

This cost per lead spreadsheet needs to be looked at on a monthly basis to make decisions to either increase or decrease your budgets per traffic source based on results. We recommend starting with a smaller test budget and then once you see pockets of profit, scale your campaigns.

By utilizing a simple cost per lead sheet by traffic source, this is how you truly hold your marketing dollars accountable.

CHAPTER SEVEN

More Secrets To Help Ensure Your Success

Now that I've shared my insider online marketing secrets, I wanted to give you some secrets that will help ensure your success even more.

SECRET #29

Compare Apples To Apples When Comparing Your Historical Data

Anytime you are comparing historical data make sure that you are comparing apples to apples. Oftentimes, when our clients start with us they are not tracking how their new patients found them.

We have seen in the past where clients have seen an increase in the number of patients from the web but their overall practice numbers seem stagnant or are even down.

When we ask how many patients they were getting from the web last year, many will not know. Without that piece of information, it is impossible to determine where the holes in their practice exist.

What we typically find when the orthodontist has a strong feeling that the web marketing is working much better but their overall numbers are pretty much the same, is that other parts of the practice are declining. Oftentimes, they are experiencing less referrals from dentists and even existing patients.

Without having the right data, we won't know for sure.

When our clients have tracked where their patients have come from previously, it is much easier to see if the web has helped them attract more new patients and ultimately fill a void of less referrals.

When you compare historical data, always make sure you are making an apple to apples comparison.

SECRET #30

Answer The Phone & Train Your Team

While this secret may seem self-explanatory and a given, based on the data we see, this secret must be included in this book. Typically, when a client first starts working with us we find one in every 5 calls goes unanswered. We also know that a new potential patient will most likely not leave a message when no one answers the phone. Instead, they will hang up and move onto the next orthodontist who does answer the phone.

When you are investing in marketing and advertising, you must answer the phone.

Additionally, you need to train your team and script out how your team should answer the phone, not only for compliance but to help turn more new patient phone calls into appointments.

SECRET #31

Follow-Up & Confirm The Initial Appointment

With referrals from dentists or other patients, typically the show-up rate for a patient to come to their initial booked appointment is fairly high. When you are attracting people into the practice who don't really know you, ideally you will send them a welcome letter or package in the mail before their initial appointment.

This helps give a great first impression and continue to build trust. Be sure to include testimonials from patients in this initial mailing because social proof will help you get more potential patients to show up to their initial appointment.

At a minimum, your team should confirm the initial appointment via phone or text. Ideally, you will reach out via the mail, too.

SECRET #32

Have Marketing Material For Absent Decision Makers

While you obviously want all decision makers to come to the initial appointment, oftentimes that doesn't happen. You should have marketing material available for the absent decision maker so they can properly learn about why you are the best and logical choice for treatment.

Beyond the typical brochure and marketing collateral, you could invite them to watch a webinar replay or video on your website which informs them about you, your process and why you are different. This information is also helpful for the people who want to review and learn more before they make their final decision.

SECRET #33

Surround Yourself With Successful People

One of my favorite quotes is by Jim Rohn, one of the world's greatest motivational speakers, "You are the average of the five people you spend the most time with."

The people you are around matter. Imagine if you are in an environment where everything is negative, fairly quickly you become more negative.

Personally, I have found going to business and marketing conferences to be a great place to surround yourself with like-minded people. On the following pages you will see pictures of me with some of the great people I have been blessed to meet. When I started going to these events and meeting these successful and famous celebrities, my mindset automatically grew. I highly recommend you attend events and surround yourself with successful, positive people.

Me with marketing legend Dan Kennedy hanging out
together in Disney World. Dan Kennedy leads the world's
largest direct response marketing organization, GKIC.

Me on the set before my interview with Jack Canfield,
the co-creator of the *Chicken Soup for the Soul* book series,
with over 500 million copies sold.
You can watch the interview at
www.JimmyMarketing.com.

Me with Emmy award-winner Leeza Gibbons before our
TV interview. In the interview, she introduced me as the
founder of, "Jimmy Marketing, America's most trusted
marketing team." You can watch the interview at
www.JimmyMarketing.com.

Me with original shark Kevin Harrington
from ABC's hit TV Show, Shark Tank.

Behind the scenes during a TV interview with Kevin
Harrington. In this interview, Kevin said, "Not only do
Jimmy Marketing websites look great, but they perform
great, too... Especially for doctors!" You can watch the
interview at www.JimmyMarketing.com.

Me with Shark Tank investor, Barbara Corcoran.

Me with ABC Secret Millionaire, James Malinchak, at his
house before a mastermind.

Me with Hall of Fame Dallas Cowboy, Emmit Smith.

Me with Bruce Buffer, official Octagon announcer
for UFC events.

Me with Joe Sugarman, founder of BluBlocker Sunglasses
and famous marketing copywriter.

Me with Brian Tracy, business advisor and
author of over 70 business books.

Me with Rudy Ruettiger,
the inspiration for the film, Rudy.

Me with Lee Cockerell,
former executive Vice President of Operations for Walt
Disney World® Resort where he led a team of 40,000 cast
members.

Me with John Assaraf from the hit movie, "The Secret."

Me with NFL MVP and Super Bowl XVII winner, Joe
Theismann.

Me hanging out with Joe Theismann before I introduced
him on stage at an event.

Me taking a question from the audience while interviewing
American actress, author, singer, businesswoman and
health spokesperson Suzanne Somers.

Me with Dr. Dustin Burelson flying private to a small
mastermind we put on together. Dr. Burleson consults to
over 1,900 orthodontists in over 24 different countries.

SECRET #34

Invest In Yourself

Another one of my favorite quotes is by Warren Buffet, one of the world's greatest investors, "The most important investment you can make is in yourself."

I have found investing in continuing education in multiple forms to be very beneficial for our growth and also our clients' growth. Moreover, we share what we learn when we attend conferences, masterminds and consume in information products with our clients.

By investing in yourself and with the right mentors and consultants you can shortcut your path to success.

I recommend you attend events, participate in masterminds and hire the right consultants so you can grow easier and faster which ultimately means you are able to help more patients.

Me with other top entrepreneurs at Dan Kennedy's house during a private mastermind.

We also got to see some of Kennedy's race horses that day.

And enjoy a great dinner together where shared even more marketing secrets.

I even got to ride in one of Dan's trotter's carts.

CHAPTER EIGHT

3 STEPS TO MY "BOOK YOURSELF SOLID" MARKETING SYSTEM

Now that I've shared my insider web marketing secrets and some success secrets, I wanted to give you a simple summary of the system. Keep in mind there are hundreds of steps we take for our clients in order to implement these three steps as profitably as possible.

Step # 1 – Ensure your website positions you as the logical and only choice for orthodontic treatment in your market. Your website must have the right messaging, right initial irresistible offer and be extremely easy to use. Your website is the foundation and key component to all of your marketing. Even word of mouth referrals go onto your website.

Step #2 – Use as many profitable traffic sources to attract more of your ideal prospects to your website.

Step #3 – Test multiple ads with tracking so with that data you can tweak your ads and website to get better and better results. Ultimately, you must hold your marketing dollars accountable for scalable and profitable growth.

CHAPTER NINE

BONUS #1 – INTERVIEW WITH DR. BURLESON & JIMMY NICHOLAS

Below you will find a transcript to a recent interview Dr. Burleson had with Jimmy Nicholas. Dr. Burleson coaches and consults to over 1,900 orthodontists in over 24 countries.

Dustin:	All right. Welcome everyone. This is Dustin Burleson from Burleson Seminars. We have a very special guest here today. This is going out to all of our clients in preparation for the upcoming customer service summit. A lot of you are registered for that. A lot of you aren't though, or you've got spring break, or you've got some other meeting with your kids, so as an added benefit to our members, we are bringing on guest

experts, and today we're very, very lucky. I've got Jimmy Nicholas on the line with me today.

We're going to talk a lot about marketing today. I assume a lot of you already heard of Jimmy, but the reality is, every month there's new clients that come, and land in this world, and are now finally being exposed to things that they probably never learned in dental school, things that they never learned in residency, so Jimmy Nicholas and I met- I'll let him share that story, but we met years ago in a marketing competition, where Jimmy kicked my butt, and he did rightfully so. We started thinking, and digging around with, could we build better websites for orthodontists? You probably heard my story. Before I found Jimmy, I was maybe getting five or 10 new patients a month from Google, or our online marketing.

In other words, Yahoo, Bing, even Facebook, and social media. It really wasn't on our radar screen at all, because our offices see hundreds and hundreds of new patients every month. Today, fast forward, Jimmy helps us get 5 to 10 new patients every day. Google has gone from the low end of our referral sources, all the way up to the top, and I think you've probably seen that as well in your practices, the power of online search. There's no one on the planet that has done more for orthodontists in putting new patients into orthodontic practices than Jimmy Nicholas, so I'm very, very honored to have him here.

Jimmy, thanks for coming on the call.

Jimmy: Thanks for inviting me back. I really appreciate it.

Dustin: I kind of led in with ... you and I, this is our world. We eat, live, and breathe new patient generation, and we're always testing new headlines, and we're always tracking our results, and we're listening to new patient phone calls. You and I kind of fly all over the world teaching orthodontists how to do this, so I kind of assumed that everyone knows who the heck you are, but the reality is, there's probably a lot of orthodontists, and dentists on the call today who are listening either in their car, or at the gym, or they've got this on their phone, or they're at the office on a Saturday getting some work done.

They've never heard of you, believe it or not, which is shocking. Maybe, tell us a little bit about who you are, what you do, and bring everyone up to speed.

Jimmy: Sure, sure. I lead a company called Jimmy Marketing, and I started basically back in 1997. I was a sophomore in high school, 15 years old, and very entrepreneurial, whether it was baseball card shows, or cutting grass, or paper route, very, very entrepreneurial. In 1997, the internet was starting to take off. Certainly, it wasn't anywhere near what it is today, but there was a Yellow Pages book sitting on my desk, and for some reason I was compelled to start calling businesses, and asking if they needed a website. At the time, I really didn't know that much about websites, but I figured I could figure it out if I could get someone to say yes to me in building them a website.

About 250 calls into it, before getting hung up on again, someone said, "Can you come over and give me a presentation, right now?" and I was so excited that the guy didn't hang up on me. I said, "Absolutely!" But I was 15, so it's not like I was going to be able to drive myself over there. Then, I had to go sell my mother on driving me over, and she waited in the car for over a couple hours while I sold this website. As a result of selling that website, in the first meeting, which was amazing. We built out the website and learned about web hosting. When you build the website, you have to put it somewhere.

So, I built a web design and web hosting business, mainly using Google AdWords all through high school and college, and then when I graduated from Bryant University in 2003, I wanted to offer more marketing services, and really diversify. I started building a team, and seeking out information, and that's where our paths crossed, in some very, very high level master mind meetings, initially, and then we ended up competing for that marketer of the year competition, and as a result of, literally, you sending that congratulatory note when I won, I was just blown away, and continuing to cross paths in these master mind meetings. We had that dinner that one night, and I was sharing with you what we were doing for podiatrists, and we were seeing that they were tripling their leads from the web, and just by following three simple steps.

Your response to me was, "Can you do that for orthodontists?" and I was obviously very, very honest, as I always am, and I said, "I don't know." and that was kind of an answer you've never heard before.

Dustin: Yeah. I was with Jimmy, if you haven't heard that story. It's the first person I've ever asked, "Will this work?" and Jimmy's like, "Well, I don't know. We'll have to test it," which was the exact correct answer, and the opposite of every other marketing firm for orthodontists. I'm not going to name names, but all the people who build websites, they're really just interested in whether or not your credit card's going to go through when they charge you 20 or 30 grand for a website, and that's the last you hear from them.

To update the sites, it's a pain in the rear end. If you called and said, "Show me the results," they can't show you the results. Yeah, because everyone else if you go and say, "Hey, can you build me a website? Will it work?" they're like, "Oh, yeah. Everyone's online, of course it's going to work. This is what you need," and Jimmy was the first person to say, "Well, I don't know. We'll test it."

Fast forward to today, I don't know anyone doing more Google Ads spend, more generation of new patient phone calls than you for orthodontists. All of our top clients use you, and we'll talk later that you can only work with one orthodontist in a specific area, which I think is smart. Also, the opposite of every other web firm, right? Every other web firm for orthodontists and dentists just rubber stamps a website for you. They don't really understand direct response marketing, because they've never actually done it. If you listen to what Jimmy just said ... He's been building websites since Al Gore invented the internet.

He's been building websites since 96, 97. Back when most of you didn't know what the World Wide Web was, and he actually eats his own cooking. In other words, he builds and buys media, and pays for AdWords for his own business, where the other big dumb companies, that I won't name names, that build websites for people in the orthodontics space, they've never actually sat down, and had to pay real money to get the phones to ring for an orthodontic practice like Jimmy has done for his own firm. We're actually in the trenches doing it, so it's kind of cool, and it's why it's been a wonderful relationship.

I'm done having kids, but I always joke, if I ever was going to have another one I would name the next one Jimmy, because that's how critical you've been to our success.

I want to give everyone listening some things that they can take home, and actually do. I think anything worth learning changes the way you see the world, and changes the way you do things. My joke is, we're not here to entertain you, we're here to see your practice grow. I want to dig into, what are the big mistakes ... I always have residents who ask, "What's the one thing?" I know there's no one thing, but what are the biggest mistakes, maybe two to three things, you see orthodontists doing when it comes to building an online presence, marketing online. So an orthodontist listening to this goes, alright, I'm going to do this. I'm going to fix my website. I'm going to start getting.

If you're really honest, and you go back and look at like, crap we only got three patients last month from Google. How do I turn that into 30? What are the biggest mistakes you see orthodontists doing when that switch finally goes off in their head?

Jimmy:	Absolutely. Let me start with a tactical strategy that everyone can do, and everyone should do, and constantly do it, and that is the logo test. The first part of our three step process is making sure that the website is right, and we're finding today that everyone online ... everyone is going online, typically before calling the orthodontist, and even word of mouth referrals, or referrals from dentists, if you're still getting referrals, they're going online. You want to make sure that that website is right, and one of the tests that we use is the logo test. What that simply is, is if you go on your website, and you take off your logo, and you replace a competitor's logo, does the information on the website still hold true? You really want to focus in on the first part of the screen, as well as on mobile devices before they have to scroll, because that's your most vital real estate on the web.

A majority of our clients, even the ones who come to us, and they just had their website redone by a local vendor, maybe another company that does orthodontic websites, they come to us, and we've got to tweak the website. In some cases we can just make some small modifications, and most cases we want to overhaul it, but we look at that, and see what could make the most sense.

The number one mistake that I see orthodontists overall making is not differentiating themselves and making themselves unique so that when that mom comes to that website she knows she's in the right place, and she wants to look a little bit further, potentially call right away, or the other scenario is, they come to a website, you look like everyone else, and it's like, well, I don't know if I should call this person or not, and they don't really have that great feeling, and they hit the back button and leave.

Number one, we've got to make sure that that website is right. The other big mistake, and I'm sure you see this as well in all of your coaching and master minding with some of your clients is the mindset challenges towards marketing. We'll have situations where we are profitably attracting new patients in through, say, a source of Google AdWords, and we know that, because we're tracking every single call that comes in through a unique dynamic tracking number that changes on the website based on where that person came from, and then we listen to every call.

There's so many companies out there that provide call tracking, and they give you a total call count, and that's really a meaningless number because it varies from practice to practice, in terms of ... of those calls that come into your practice, how many are actual leads, and how many of them are turning into appointments? Because of the tracking, we're able to determine exact ROI on a traffic source. So, with Google, the lowest hanging fruit are people who are searching for braces, for Invisalign, for an orthodontist, and if you have the opportunity to be there on Google, you would definitely want to take advantage of that.

These are people who are going to be the easiest patients to say yes to your treatment because they're actively searching for it. We'll have situations where the client could invest more dollars into more traffic, but they don't, because of some number that they feel is like their budget. That number in their head is their limit that they're going to invest in Google, no matter what. The story that comes to mind with this is, through many emails and calls our team convinced one of our clients to invest more dollars into Google AdWords, and the next week got a family of three to come in, and sign up for treatment through Google.

If that mom had searched, and that orthodontist was limited by budget and never even showed up, he would have missed out on three cases because of that. When you find that profitable traffic source, and you know it's profitable, and you have the ability to scale it to more, you have to invest and not look at marketing as an expense, but a true investment so you can help more patients.

Dustin: Yeah. The mindset is huge. We have so many clients who will assume that parents will just find them because they're such a good orthodontist. That might have been true in the 1960's, when there were three orthodontists in your town, right, but there's more and more orthodontists opening. There are more and more general dentists doing orthodontics, especially with Invisalign. Now, we've got direct to consumer aligners with Smile Direct Club, and there'll be more competitors that enter that space as well. I just have kind of gotten harsh with clients. You've probably heard me say, or they've heard me say like, oh.

It came in one master mind that this particular client was.... It's kind of playing devil's advocate a little bit, but it came to the point where the rubber had to meet the road, and we had to get a result for his office, and it was this same mindset issue of, you basically want something for nothing. That's just not how the marketplace works. You don't get something for nothing. You don't get to say, "I want to build the practice by a million bucks," and then shy away from a ten thousand dollar investment in Google AdWords. It's just not how it works.

Now, in some markets it might be a couple thousand dollars, but I'm shocked the number of millionaire orthodontists. These guys doing one million, two million bucks a year in their practice, and I had this conversation privately with Dan Kennedy He's like, I mean, they're doing two million bucks a year, and they're just whining and complaining about marketing, and they're spending a thousand bucks a month, or we had one client spending two thousand dollars a year in a very competitive market, basically doing no marketing, and still doing $1.2 million.

Dan's like, "There's no other business like this on the planet."
Financial advisors, restaurant owners, salons, daycare centers, their jaws would drop if they knew what most orthodontists spend on marketing, how little it is, and the results that they're getting.

Thank God we're in a wonderful profession that people value what we do, but it is amazing. We're like, "Well, I'm just going to spend X, and whenever we're done spending X just turn off my Google Ad-Words." That's the most insane thing I've ever heard. We're just like, "Well, I just want to make a hundred thousand bucks this month, so as soon as we hit that number, just close the office." It's the fifth day of the month, you've hit your goal, you're just going to close the rest of the month? It's just not how smart business owners think. Yeah. I would agree. I would totally second your assessment that a lot of this starts in the heads of orthodontists who've never had to really make any significant marketing investments before.

What we know is true is that you're either going to have to get serious about your marketing, or you're going to be swallowed whole by those who do. All right, so Invisalign recently said they are going to launch their most aggressive campaign ever directed at teenagers, Smile Direct Club ... These are companies that have six, seven hundred million bucks cash in the bank. I think Invisalign has about seven hundred million dollars cash in the bank. If you're not playing this game of how do we capture new patients when they start their search online, and on mobile, you're really, really, really behind the eight ball, and it's time to start to take it seriously.

Tell me ... You obviously worked with tons and tons and tons of our clients. There might be someone listening who's trying to figure out, do I do this myself? Do I hire someone like Jimmy? Do I hire my nephew who knows how to build websites? Who is, or who isn't ... I guess, maybe we'll go that way. Obviously, not everyone's a good client for you. Everyone's not ideal. Who's not a good client for Jimmy Marketing?

Jimmy: Going back to the mindset. You really have to have an open mindset to trying and testing new ads, new copy in ads. We'll help craft the ads, and we'll actually share with you ads that are working well for other orthodontists throughout the country.

We've built a software system that allows us to literally take in all the ads that we're managing for orthodontists, and it spits out the winning ads for us each month, and for the clients listening to the call, we'll be sharing that ... those with you in an offline environment, because we do want to keep that information very, very secure, but having that open mindset to even maybe testing platforms that you've tried before.

If you've tried Google AdWords before and it didn't work for you, maybe you did it a different way, or maybe you had that same poor messaging that was on your website that really didn't differentiate you. The open mindset is critical, and I would say, we're not for the orthodontist who's just looking to get a few new patients. If you're comfortable, and you're not really looking to dominate your market and help as many new patients as possible, we're probably not the right fit because what I like to do is, is I like to see the data. I like to see the profit coming in from these different traffic sources, and then scale it up. When we come to you, my team comes to you as a client and says, "Hey. We can increase the Google AdWords budget." That conversation needs to be an exciting conversation, not, oh my gosh, I've got to increase my marketing expenses.

It's really very key that you have that right mindset, in terms of that growth mindset, and realize that you need to invest in order to get your message out so that your potential patients know who you are. It really comes down to the mindset, and the willingness to do what needs to be done in order to grow your practice.

Dustin: Yeah. I used to be surprised by this, but I've been doing this long enough now, with enough orthodontists that—I'm not trying to be rude to people that might be listening to the call, because there are legitimately clients who just say, you know what—I had this private call about two weeks ago, and this client is just being slow on getting things implemented, and I say, "Help me understand. Why aren't you doing this?" The more I chipped away at it, because a lot of times I'd play therapist on the phone with these clients. They're complaining about this, that, and the other, and he just opened up and said, "I really don't want to work that much harder."

You hit the nail on the head. If you really just want to stay where you are, or grow incrementally then yeah, I wouldn't put your toe in the water with this, but I used to assume everyone thinks the way you and I think, which is like, grab it by the horns, and wrestle it to the ground. I used to joke, but I'm not really joking anymore. I don't want my competitors kids to starve, but I don't think they got to eat that much. I'm fine if a few of them pack up and leave town. That's how everyone that grows a big business thinks, and it is harsh, but this is for big girls and big boys.

Steve Jobs said, "I want to put a ding in the universe," and on his death bed said, "I'll spend Apple's last penny fighting Google Android." Gates was notoriously aggressive. Bezos is notoriously aggressive. Warren Buffett looks peaceful and calm on the outside when he's on CNBC. I can promise you he's extremely aggressive in the deals that he negotiates. If you really just want to grow by a little bit, and again, I'm not trying to be offensive, because some people do. I've had clients say, "Listen, I don't want to be you. I don't want to have multiple locations. Can I grow at a steady pace?" Yes, but this isn't really a conversation for you if you want to maintain a status quo. If you don't want to put a moat around your practice, and really compete, or protect yourself from competitors. This really isn't for you.

When I get a call from you, or from my marketing strategist at Jimmy Marketing, I get a phones report every day. I see what we're doing. I've got to make decisions now on, do we ramp this up? Where are we? What day is it in the month? How have we now achieved the goals that we should have achieved by that day in the month? No orthodontist should have ... With this type of technology, no orthodontists should have a bad month. You should have a bad half day, and then you should go fix it, because you can really dial this up and down. Right now, right now, if you're listening to us on a Sunday or on a Saturday, right now, there is a mom in your town looking for an orthodontist that she is going to call this week, or maybe get in touch with right now if you have the ability to do that.

The question is, are you positioned where your practice will get that mom to call you first? I just think it is true. This is like ... really a mindset lecture that we're getting into, but it's fascinating to me, and I'm not surprised by it anymore. The number of orthodontists that just want to go fishing on Friday, and who really don't have the ambition to go and double the practice, or triple the practice, because they've become comfortable, but if you go back to when you started the business, at one point, you grew it like 10X, you took it from nothing to a million. So, there's nothing stopping you from doing that again. There's a great article I read about the guy ... the My Pillow guy. The only thing standing between him and a billion dollars is how much media he can buy, because he's got a system that works, and that's exactly what Jimmy's system does.

We can just dial it up. If we think we need another 20 new patients, we can increase the ads spend, test a few more ads, make sure the phones are covered, and schedule the patients. I totally agree. Huge mindset shift. You've been doing this for a while. I know a lot of clients ... There might be, probably, a lot of clients listening who are already clients of yours, and they're always looking for the next new thing. On the flip side of that coin, where a lot of orthodontists just want to go fishing, I think in Burleson Seminars we attract a lot of orthodontists who think exactly the opposite.

They want to go chase down big goals. What have you learned about marketing for orthodontists now, today, that you didn't know when we first hired you many moons ago?

Jimmy: Actually, a lot, because before working with you, and the many orthodontists that we work with now, our three step system was working in other industries. While the system is transferable to pretty much any industry that we've tested, it has seen great results with it. We really have had the opportunity, over the years in working with you and many of your coaching clients, to hone down the messaging, and really test new messages, and find out what's working, what's not working, and the amount of data that we have available to us today compared to when we first started is amazing.

We're able to spy on what Invisalign is doing from an advertising standpoint online. What Smile Direct Club is doing. What the competitor in your local backyard is doing, and we're also able to see what people are typing into the search engines

and how they're finding you. We're
able to look at long tail keyword
phrases where not everyone will just
put in orthodontist, and the town
name, and the state. It is a big part,
but a lot of people will type in
braces for my child, and orthodontist for adults, longer tail keyword
phrases, and we're able to see which
ones are clicked the most, and which
ones are getting the most interest,
which then allows us to update ads.
Maybe create a blog article specific
around that keyword phrase, which
is going to increase your rankings
with Google.

A few years ago, when we were
starting, we didn't have all of this
data that we have today, and we certainly didn't have this system that I
built to manage all of the data and
see what's coming in, in terms of
number of calls and leads, and leads
that turn into appointments. It's really at our fingertips, but it's also ...
because of the amount of data, we
need to know which data to look at,
and then how to apply what we're
learning into, basically, profits. Profitability to help increase, and attract
more new patients into the practice,
because you could just look at data
all day long and not take action, or
really not even know what data

you're supposed to be looking at. There's just so much of it.

Dustin: That's what every orthodontist does with their end of the month reports, which I say are pretty much useless. All right, because it's a historical record of what's already happened. I'm way more interested in what's going on right now, or what patients are telling you based on their action. Number of phone calls, time of day of those phone calls, which ads are getting those phone calls, the questions they ask. Are you listening to the phone calls? All of those data allow us to predict, and make decisions moving forward. That's why I love this media, as much as I'm an old curmudgeon when it comes to it. I love direct mail. I love direct response radio.

I love cable TV. I love magazines, and we're still in the newspaper for crying out loud, and they all work, but for direct mail, the fastest that I can pivot is 30 days, because we've got to get the campaign in the mail. Then, I've got to wait for the expiration date of those offers, listen to the phone calls, wait for all of those post cards to come back with a tear off coupon or a tear off gift card, and in 30 days I learn something, but with your system I could learn today. I get lunch, I can learn what happened with the ads we changed yesterday, really, really cool, let's us pivot, let's us react much quicker.

Which takes me to my next topic. The hit list of things I think that orthodontists need to leave this call with, which I hope you're taking notes by the way, is I still see a lot of orthodontists not doing retargeting, and I think a lot of orthodontists don't know what retargeting is, but talking about the nimble nature, and the ability to pivot, and the ability to do things with this media that we can't do with other media is that we can find the people most likely to respond to our ads in our market, bring them to our website, bring them into an ad, and then retarget them over, and over, and over again.

So, talk about that, talk about—I still think for how inexpensive it is, I'm shocked there aren't more orthodontists doing it.

Jimmy: Absolutely. Let me explain quickly what retargeting is, for those of you who maybe ... I'm sure you've seen it, but maybe you're not aware, oh, that's retargeting. So, what it is, is if you go onto a website that is setup with retargeting, when you leave that website you'll see an ad throughout the internet, and it will be the ad that, branding wise, matches your website. Maybe it's a link to a blog article, or free report, or some more branding for you, and you could imagine the potential mom who comes to your website, and then leaves, because sometimes it takes time for a mom to decide if this is the orthodontist to call or not call, or she gets distracted.

The baby is in the house, and something happens, and she gets distracted, and somehow gets off your website before calling you. Well, with retargeting, they will see your ad over the next few weeks, all over the internet for pennies, and literally ... usually our retargeting budgets are a hundred to two hundred dollars a month for our clients, and what that enables you to have is that omnipresent feel, that top of mind awareness feel, and your ads will show up on some major websites like Time Magazine, or CNBC we've seen ads on, or a local newspaper.

You could go to that newspaper, sign up for advertising for probably five hundred to five thousand dollars a month. We're able to get you on that paper, not just anywhere on the paper, or to anyone who's reading that paper, to the people who have been to your website, the hottest people, and they'll see you advertised there. Perhaps it's a blog that the mom reads, her favorite mommy blog, and there's your ad, and now you're building rapport, because you're there in her world. Retargeting is such an easy thing to do if you know what you're doing. I don't expect an orthodontist to know how to set up retargeting, but for us, and for marketing companies that are out there it's a very easy thing to implement.

Sometimes we hear, well, I find retargeting to be annoying, and I don't want you to put yourself in your shoes in how you shop online when it comes to what your mindset is, I want you to put yourself in your potential patients' shoes, and how they would go about searching, and put your own feelings and what you're thinking aside, because it's more important if we can help you attract more patients who don't necessarily know you, and if they see your ad throughout the internet they get to know you more. You've heard the study, they range from ... they have to see you five times to a hundred times, or even more before they actually feel that trust, and hear your name, and see your logo, and feel that trust factor. Obviously, with any-thing, medical certainly, braces, Invisalign, things in the mouth, that trust needs to be there.

So, retargeting is something that you definitely want to make sure that you have implemented for your practice.

Dustin: Yeah. I want to touch on ... for the or-thodontists listening, your feelings about all of this don't matter. The only thing that matters are the results. If messenger pigeons were still the best way to get our marketing mes-sage to prospective new patients, I would use messenger pigeons, even though my personal feeling about messenger pigeons is that they would probably crap all over the place, be a pain in the ass to feed, and be a real nightmare logistically, and with liabil-ity of who knows what happens sending out messenger pigeons.

It's not about my feelings about it. I have so many clients who just like you said, well, retargeting is kind of annoying. Right, like we had a client say, well, I just feel like direct mail is tacky. Well, I don't care what your feelings about it are, or my patients are too sophisticated for direct mail, or my patients are going to be an-noyed by retargeting. Well, when you show me the data ... if you go invest six figures in retargeting and give me ten years' worth of data on it, then we can have a conversation.

That's different than your feelings about it. To that client I said, "Well, if direct mail is tacky. I'm going to name some companies, you tell me if you think these companies are tacky." These are all companies that spend millions, tens of millions, Google spends a hundred million dollars a year on direct mail, Nordstrom, Apple, Disney, The Four Seasons, Ritz-Carlton, Harley Davidson, Mercedes Benz; are these tacky companies? These are some of the largest direct mail marketers in the world.

Now, let's play the retargeting game. Well, retargeting is annoying. Okay, who else is doing retargeting? Oh crap, Apple, Four Seasons, Disney. It doesn't really matter what you feel, or how you think your patients are going to perceive retargeting. The only thing that matters is the results, and I will tell you for very little money per month, we see patients coming to us from the Kansas City Star, where if I go, and try to negotiate with the Kansas City Star—I tell you, because we do, we have online ... it's about 15 hundred bucks a

week if I want to blast everyone, but
with someone smart like Jimmy, I
can just target the people who have
already searched for me, already
looked for me, already been to my
website, already been to my Facebook page, and I might spend 45
dollars that week, or that month.

It really doesn't matter how you feel
about it without being too offensive.
The only thing that matters is the results. One day—I always joke and
say, one day Jimmy and I, when
we've retired, we will sit in the backyard, overlooking the lake with a
glass of wine, and we will theorize
and pontificate on why certain
things work, or why retargeting was
so powerful, but until then all we
care about is that we get the results.
I really don't care why it works, how
it works, I don't even know how to
set it up.

If Jimmy put a gun to my head and
said go set up your retargeting, and I
wouldn't know how to do it. I just
know that it works. I know that the
more money I put into it the better
results we get, and I know that
Jimmy knows how to do it, so I put
his team in charge of it. Cool. All
right, I just wanted to hammer that
point home, because it really doesn't
matter what we think about it. The

results are all that matter. Okay. I know you've been working with a lot of our clients. I know we talked a little bit about what's holding them back with heir mindset. Tell me a little bit about why an orthodontist would pull his or her punches, and not do something like this outside of their mindset?

Jimmy: I mean, I think it really comes down to fear. Human nature is constantly to self-doubt yourself. What if I invest all of this money, and no one comes, or what if I hire another web company ... what if I hire Jimmy Marketing, and I had this previous bad experience with one or maybe multiple companies, and how do I know it's not going to be the same. It's this constant fear that's holding them back, and if they can get through that, and get to a yes, where yeah, Jimmy Marketing can help you. Do we know if it's going to work for you? No, we don't.

It's the same answer that I gave you, Dr. Burleson, when we were talking about it, but today we do have great stats, we have ... of the clients who have started with us, over a 95% retention ratio, so they're staying. I'd like to mention, obviously, with the Customer Service Summit coming up. Yeah, we provide great customer service, but at the end of the day it comes down to the results, because if the results aren't there than you're not going to be able to invest in ads, invest in us. It's breaking through that fear to get to the yes, and basically put their trust in our system to test it out.

As you know, not every time are we going to turn this on and get a hundred new patients in a month, but we're going to get some data, we're going to look at it, we're going to make modifications, and we're going to get better, and better, and better. It's a real honest approach, and realistic approach to marketing, and when you look at the risk reward factor, in terms of not working ... leveraging your web marketing as best as you can, and how much money you're leaving on the table. How many patients are you losing that are going to your competitors, or you could get your web marketing right ... working for you 24/7 as best as possible, and help more patients.

Seeing the difference in those scenarios, the risk reward is really a low risk, too. Especially in the orthodontist industry, because the case values are five thousand to eight thousand, some of our clients

11 thousand, and if ... you don't need many new patients, and if we're tracking everything, we can prove that it is a great return on investment for you. When it comes to fear, we've implemented a two-part guarantee ... money back guarantee where the first part of what we're doing is we're working on the website.

At any point before going live with the website, or if we're working with your existing site making tweaks, if you don't think we're the right fit, you can ask for your money back, and we'll give you a hundred percent of your money back based on what you've invested with us to that date. Once that site's live, now we go into the marketing phase, and typically we'll test together for three months, and then at that three month mark we're going to determine if you want to continue with us on a month to month basis, or take it over yourself, or part ways.

What we're willing to do is, on our side, in terms of what you're paying Jimmy Marketing to set everything up, optimize everything, work with you, listen to all of the calls, do all of the SEO, help you with the reviews, everything that we do for those three months if you feel that we're not the right company, and you want to part ways after that three months, and you felt like we didn't do a good job at it, and you want your money back, ask for your money back, and we'll give you a hundred percent of our service fee for those three months back to you.

Dustin: Nobody does that, and transparency, to people listening, if not every day, every week there's some company that wants to get in front of our clients, so we've built a very large list of orthodontists that pay attention to us every week through the Burleson Report, or every week through the weekly fax, or every month they'll look over my shoulder, and without tooting our horn too much we've built the largest orthodontic consulting firm on the planet. We're in 25 countries. Every week there's someone who wants to get in front of our clients.

We do financial advising. Let me talk, let's do a webinar. We do websites, we do social media, we do offline media, we do staff training, we sell equipment, we sell braces, everything, we sell software, everybody wants to get in front of our clients. We've only put a handful of people in front of our clients for the exact reason Jimmy just mentioned.

Two things that he won't brag on about himself, but I will, is that 95% of his clients stay with him long term. If you look at the industry average, hitting a home run is 80 to 85%. That means most web firms, two things they do, they make you sign a ridiculous contract that will make you pay through the nose to get out of, and the minute that contract is up, 50% of those clients drop.

That's the average. Long term retention with website hosting companies, website marketing companies, is they sign you to a very long contract, 12 months, 24 months, and the minute that contract is up, because of all the reasons we listed, right, that it's a pain in the butt to get the site updated, no one's looking at long tail keyword searches, no one's actually updating you on phone calls, you get your head screwed on straight, and go like, crap, I'm spending a lot of money on this website, and it's not producing any results for me. So, the minute you can get out, you get out, and half the clients drop, and they go somewhere else.

This is in dentistry, it's in orthodontics, it's in websites across the board. The fact that Jimmy's clients, 95% stay with him long term is the best, no one can match that. Second, is no one gives a money back guarantee, because I know what it takes to run Jimmy's firm. I've seen his team, it's huge. He's got people that work with him in Connecticut. He's got people that work with him in Florida, all over the country, all over the world, and it's like 50, 60 people that run this thing, and he's got to pay them to build your stuff. That's unprecedented. There's no web firm—you can go tomorrow, and shop around to people who build orthodontic websites, and say, what happens if I don't like it, and we're halfway in, and I want to change my mind, they laugh, right. No one does that.

It ties in perfectly with the customer service summit, which is where Jimmy's going to be joining us in Kansas City, and it is why he is in front of our clients, because we only put people in front of our orthodontists who provide great customer service. Thanks for doing that, which is ... you won't brag on you, but I'll brag on you. Wrapping up in a few minutes, I'd like to leave, but first I want to make sure everyone has a chance to find you, and to learn more about you, because I think everyone should, but take me to where you see digital marketing in the next two to five years, because man it has changed since we met, like every day I feel like I'm learning something new, and I'm so glad you're like ... the analogy I use is like ... it's like being on a golf course you've never played before, and Jimmy's the world's best caddy, and he's going to show you everywhere to go, and every club to use, and every place to hit, and get you through the course successfully.

How do you see the digital marketing landscape changing in the next maybe two, three, four, five years, and what should orthodontists be doing now to prepare for that?

Jimmy: Absolutely. It's a great question, and we'll go into the crystal ball, into the future, and we were right in predicting mobile is where it's going. We predicted that a few years ago, and now we're seeing more than half of traffic going on mobile devices. In terms of where see it going from here, I see a lot of media segmentation going to start. You've got Google, you've got Facebook, but you also have these micro blogs, and special interest websites, and forums, and I see people, just like the media has become segmented with

TV, in terms of the number of channels. I mean, you've got to compete with Tivo, and are they even going to see the ad? That sort of stuff.

I see the media online becoming more, and more segmented. When I say media I really mean the media of online ads, which is going to make tracking of everything even more and more important. I always go to your story of, you don't have one way to get a hundred patients, but you have a hundred ways to get one patient, and you use every one of them. What you want to do is take that same concept online, and get yourself multiple traffic sources, track everything, and then the ones that are working you invest more, and the ones that aren't just stop. It's using that data.

We're going to have more, and more importance of data in the coming years, and you have to prepare for it, you have to be aware of it, and know how to, and where to look for the right data, so that you can make the right decisions, so that you don't bottle neck your growth, and you actually grow the orthodontic practice.

Dustin: That's so true. If you go back to when your parents, my parents at the end of the day would turn on

Johnny Carson. He had 20, 22 million viewers every night. I think Jimmy Fallon's at like two to two point two. Colbert, now that Trump is president, has peaked a little bit, maybe two, two and a half million. It's 10% of what it used to be. The audience, the market is so fragmented, like you mentioned, that you can no longer assume you can just throw some Google AdWords up. We haven't talked about Bing and Yahoo, and really we haven't dug into ... we don't have enough time to dig into all the different ways we can use retargeting.

We haven't really had a chance to dig into how we can put different ads in front of different people based on what device they're on, and where they are. The mom, who's sitting on her couch on a Saturday afternoon, on a laptop has a very different mindset than a mom who's on a mobile phone at 11 O'clock at night at CVS looking for antibiotics for her kid's toothache. There's a whole lot people still have to learn, but I want people to understand that this one solution fits all, it's over. It's done. If you were a marketer in the 1960's, you had to worry about ABC, CBS, NBC, and then eventually in the 70's and 80's, Fox. You have four options.

There's four hundred options now on cable TV, and no one's watching it in front of their television, and everyone who is watching it with a laptop, or a tablet, or their phone, and phones have surpassed desktops, so the story I'm trying to present to you without putting you into tail spinning depression is that Jimmy's right. This will continue to get more and more complex. It will continue to get more and more fragmented, so that if you aren't doing this with someone who can help you navigate these waters, you are in a teeny tiny sailboat in the middle of a massive storm in the middle of the ocean.

I can tell you who does have this figured out is smart companies like Invisalign, Smile Direct Club, Aspen Dental, Comfort Dental. They've got millions of dollars in ad spend, and they've got smart marketing people doing this. The good news is what they think is their competitive advantage AKA being big, is really their disadvantage. You can make a decision today to hire Jimmy, to fix your website, and on Monday you can start to see that progress. You can sit down with his team, get the ball rolling, and within a few months you've got a totally different competitive advantage than all of the other orthodontists in your town who look at this, and go, well, crap, it's too complex. I don't want to compete. I guess I'll just keep doing things the way I've been doing them. I'll just maintain. They'll put their head in the sand.

That's not how smart orthodontists think. You get to pivot, and make decisions where Smile Direct Club, Invisalign, Aspen Dental they've got to go to their board. They've got to go, and it takes them a lot longer to turn the ship, and to make decisions. I think what we've taught our clients is the client must get to higher ground. There are still a ton of patients in your market who would love to come see you, that can't find their way to you, because you don't have this stuff fixed yet. I know we're getting close to being at the end of the hour. I want to make sure people get a chance to find their way to you.

First, thanks Jimmy for being here. I always take a ton of notes, and I've got a few things I want to talk to my person about. Tia is the one who helps me at your office. I've got a few things I want to send to her, because every time we talk I have an idea, and you give me an idea to go work on, so thank you. How do people find you? I know a lot of them are going to see you at the customer service summit. How do they find you? Someone who wants to find out more, where should they go?

Jimmy: Absolutely. JimmyMarketing.com is our company website. You can certainly go there, but we had prepared today a lot more information that I wanted to get to your listeners, so I think the best thing for everyone to do would be to go to www.OrthoCaseStudy.com. What you'll find there is a case study video, where I talk about the three step process, and how it worked for you, Dr. Burleson, and other orthodontists as well, you'll learn about our process, and you'll learn about Jimmy Marketing.

It's about a forty-five minute video, and you just go there www.OrthoCaseStudy.com, and you're going to learn the three step system that we didn't get to go into detail today, and I would say that would be probably the best first step that you could do, and if you've already talked to us previously and are still thinking about signing up, I would go watch that video, and just refresh yourself in what we can do for you.

Dustin: Awesome! Thank you, thank you, thank you! I will send this out if you're getting this on a physical CD in the mail, you want to look, I'll include that URL and I'll include Jimmy's contact information. If you're listening digitally, because we will send this out digitally as well. If you're listening on your device, or you got this in an email, you'll see that link in the email, the OrthoCaseStudy.com. I'll make sure I put that up for everyone. Jimmy, as always thanks for being here, you always deliver a ton of value, and I know the orthodontists that are listening, they'll want to finally take control of the new patients in their market, finding them first, no one's done that better than you. I mean that from the bottom of my heart. You've changed our practice, and you're changing the lives of orthodontists all over the world, so thank you as always for being here. I really appreciate it.

Jimmy: Thanks for having me.

Dustin: All right everyone, we will talk to you again next time. For all of you that are going to be visiting us in

Kansas City for the customer service summit, Jimmy will be there. Jimmy and I will be presenting a lot of new things that we have not presented before. There were like 10 other questions I wanted to ask you about how you built your team, and we're going to talk about that in Kansas City on how Jimmy's built an amazing team, how we are now making sure that our team of employees has a resource on our own website privately, behind a secure system that Jimmy's built for us. We're going to be digging in, and sharing a lot of that in Kansas City. There's always new stuff when you meet smart marketers like Jimmy Nicholas your world just gets bigger, and cool things happen. Jimmy, it's an honor to know you. Thanks for being here, and we'll see you in Kansas City, okay?

Jimmy: Sounds good.

Dustin: All right, buddy. Thank you.

CHAPTER TEN

BONUS #2 – HARVARD SPEECH: "ALWAYS GIVE MORE THAN YOU RECEIVE"

The Harvard Faculty Club invited me to speak to a group of entrepreneurs and students. The topic of my speech was how success comes from always giving more than you receive.

Below is the transcript of the full speech.

Harvard Business School Entrepreneur's Club, thank you for inviting me back to speak. The last time I was speaking at Harvard, it was about four years ago and I was speaking on the subject of marketing. Today, I am here to talk with you about the entrepreneur's journey.

My journey officially started when I was 15 years old. It was 1997, and the Internet was just starting to take off, and I knew every business would quickly need their own website. Now, I didn't know how to build a website, or really anything about websites, but I knew I could figure that part out.

So, there was a Yellow Pages book sitting on my desk, and for some reason I was compelled to start cold calling businesses and asking if they wanted a website. For the first 246 calls, everyone was saying they weren't interested or they were just hanging up on me. But, on that 247th call, a local jewelry store owner said, "Yes, I am interested, can you come over and give me a presentation right now?" Well, I was so excited he didn't hang up on me, I said, "Absolutely, I'll be right over." But remember, I was only 15 years old, so I had to ask my mom if she would drive me over there. Thankfully, she said yes and she waited in the car for over two hours. Her wait was so worth it because I walked out of there with a check for $1,500. I sold my first website that day.

Now, running a successful and profitable business allowed me an amazing lifestyle throughout my school years. When I graduated from Bryant University I had more time available, so I started offering more marketing services.

As I gained more and more clients I realized I needed help. So, I started hiring employees and building a team. Now, in a service-based business like a marketing agency, your business goes in cycles. There are stages where you have too much work for too few employees or too little work with too many employees. This is when I started experiencing cash flow issues. For those of you in the audience who own your own business or practice, you most likely have experienced a cash flow crunch at some point, too.

I don't know about you, but I got into business for freedom, and I found myself working well over 100 hours per week and on top of it, not only was I not making money, I was losing money. I racked up over $190,000 in credit card debt in attempts to grow the business. My relationship with my wife was on the rocks. I didn't know how I was going to make payroll, and ultimately keep the business going. I felt trapped and with no way out.

Since I had already maxed out all the credit cards, my only option was to sell more services in order to generate the cash needed to keep this big machine going that I built. Well, I was so focused on trying to make money that I forgot about the most important principle in business, which is to always give more value than what you receive.

Because my back was against the wall and the debt was either going to go away with a bankruptcy or I was going to be able to pay it all off at some point ... I stopped focusing on my debt problem, and instead I shifted all my efforts and energy on helping our clients get the best results as possible.

It was a phenomenal shift.

For example, we were able to take an orthodontist that was getting only $10,000 a month of patient production from the web, to over $282,000 a month in patient production from Google alone. As you can imagine, with getting incredible results like that, we constantly receive many referrals from that particular client and, of course, our other clients as well, which has helped Jimmy Marketing to become the successful company that it is today and with $0 in credit card debt. Yes, by following the principle of always giving more than you receive, I was able to pay off all those credit cards without going bankrupt.

I am now able to spend quality time with my beautiful wife and son and I have the freedom in my life to do exactly what I want, when I want, and the financial ability to do so.

So how does all of this relate to you?

Well, in looking back along my journey from success, to struggle, and back to success. I learned so many life and business lessons. But I want to leave you with one key business principle that is crucial for success... and that is to always give more than you receive. If you follow that principle, you will be extremely successful and you will help more people.

As always, I wish you success in all areas of your life. Thank you so much!

CHAPTER ELEVEN

Bonus #3 – Must Watch Case Study Video

I have put together a free video you can watch online by going to www.OrthoCaseStudy.com which show-cases Dr. Burleson and other orthodontists' case studies.

In this video, you will discover the three steps that will help you stop losing patients to corporate dentistry and help you predictably attract more new patients into your orthodontic practice.

CHAPTER TWELVE

WHAT'S NEXT

Well, there you have it. You have just read how to book yourself solid and catapult over your local competition to become the undisputed No. 1 orthodontist in your market.

Candidly, having told you all, I also need to tell you this: There are literally thousands of "little things" you still need to know to translate understanding into implementation and to create an automated patient attraction machine with the right ads and offers.

You see, it does not matter how successful the other orthodontists we are currently helping are.

Their successes don't pay your bills. They don't get your phone to ring. They don't give you the lifestyle and income you deserve.

The only thing that you can do is to take this information and move from knowledge to implementation. To have Jimmy Marketing help you implement this automatic patient attraction machine into your practice, I recommend you schedule a free, no-obligation marketing strategy call with one of our marketing advisors. You can schedule your call by filling out the short form at www.YourOrthoMarketingCall.com. After you fill out the form, you will be able to instantly schedule your marketing strategy call.

When I won Marketer of the Year in 2013 out of 30,000 very talented, savvy business owners worldwide, I went from obscurity to international celebrity. Business owners all over the world began calling me to work with them and share my secrets.

In the end, I chose to work almost exclusively with orthodontists. I saw how they are changing lives. I have a small son, Carter. When he smiled for the first time I knew the power of a smile. If I could take what I've worked so hard to learn and fine-tune and make a difference in people's lives through the orthodontists we work with, I considered it to be a triple win — win for the Orthodontist, win for the patient, and win for Jimmy Marketing.

This has become our overwhelming "WHY."

But we don't work with just any orthodontist.

We know that 99 percent of all success is between the ears. You must expect success and develop the right mindset, and develop your overwhelming "why" you want to grow your practice.

If you're not ready ...

If you're not committed ...

If you don't have a big enough "why" ...

If all you say is "it won't work in my practice" ...

... then all my secrets, strategies and suggestions will never help you.

One of the first things we always check also when we have a first conversation with an orthodontist is if there are any other orthodontists within their market area that we already work with. Since what we do is so powerful, so different, so unique, we will only work with one orthodontist in an area. If we worked with more, it would dilute the effectiveness for everyone in that market.

As you can tell, we are all about results.

While our system has worked for Dr. Burleson and many other orthodontists, I do want to share another story of one of our mutual clients. We worked with an orthodontist who went from $1.1 million to $2.3 million in just one year. He was ready. He was committed and he did his part by innovating his practice, providing feedback and assets when asked which all helped in more than doubling his practice. You can learn about more case studies like this by going to www.OrthoCaseStudy.com and watching the free video.

I realize with anything new, there's fear and skepticism it won't work.

We cannot guarantee every orthodontist will double his or her practice, but what I can tell you is you have three choices:

- Do nothing. Keep doing exactly what you've been doing. If you have gotten this far in this book, I highly doubt this is even a logical option for you.

- Do it all yourself. Pay a lot of money like I did to learn how to do online, direct-response marketing and, with the help of your staff and freelancers, try to get it all done.
- Let us help you. A marketing strategy call with us is free.

My Unconditional Special Offer To You

We've done hundreds of consulting calls with orthodontists; most tell us they have no idea exactly how many patients they secure from marketing strategies used by their existing vendors. And most of the time they haven't even hardly talked to the marketing companies handling their websites.

This is completely wrong and a huge disservice not only to you, but also to the patients who are going to your competition.

The reasons:
- The message is all wrong.
- The websites don't directly speak to your ideal prospect in the words that prospects want to hear.
- Marketing techniques are outdated and so ineffective.
- Results are not tracked, so it's not clear what's working and what's not.
- Their marketing eggs all go in one basket, which limits your possibilities.

- They wait for you to give them direction rather than offering innovative, professional, proven ideas.

Since we're a marketing and a strategy company – not just a website template builder company – I want to offer you a …

FREE marketing strategy call with one of our marketing advisors.   On this call you will learn …

- if you have a website that converts visitors into consultations.
- why your current website is NOT converting as many visitors into new patient phone calls as it should be.
- your clear path to more patients.
- if we can help you with your challenges.
- why we have over a 93% retention rate.
- some things that you can tweak right away .
- the critical proven elements to the Jimmy Marketing Website Blueprint and why it works.
- why you should potentially never advertise.
- why you are watering down your advertising dollars.
- why there is much more to your success than being #1 on Google.
- why exclusivity must be a standard in today's competitive marketplace.
- why your web marketing vendor has to go way beyond just building your website and managing your SEO and online ads.
- if you really have a problem with your website.

Again, this marketing strategy call is 100% no obligation. This is not a sales call in disguise and you can leave your credit card in your wallet for this marketing strategy call... Guaranteed!

www.YourOrthoMarketingCall.com

Just the fact that you've read this far says you're not an ordinary orthodontist.

We'd love to connect with you and hear how you used the information in this book to get yourself booked solid.

www.YourOrthoMarketingCall.com

We look forward to talking with you soon! As always, we wish you the best of success!

Made in the USA
Middletown, DE
30 October 2019